# John Quincy Adams and
# American Continental Empire

Walter LaFeber was born in Walkerton, Indiana, and studied at Hanover College, Stanford University, and The University of Wisconsin. His first book, *The New Empire: An Interpretation of American Expansion, 1865-1898,* received the Albert J. Beveridge Prize as the best manuscript submitted to the American Historical Association in 1962. He is at present Associate Professor of History at Cornell University.

# John Quincy Adams AND American Continental Empire

LETTERS, PAPERS AND SPEECHES

*edited by Walter LaFeber*

CHICAGO

*Quadrangle Books*

1965

Library of Congress Catalog Card Number: 65-12780.

Manufactured in the United States of America.

Designed by Lawrence Levy.

# PREFACE

This book attempts to reveal to the reader the mind of America's greatest Secretary of State. Diplomatic history here becomes a great man's personal passions and prejudices, his unique and sweeping views of how the world's political, economic, and ideological systems operated, and his fervent belief in the future magnificence of an American continental empire.

In compiling an inexpensive edition of Adams' writings, I have been more concerned with motivation than with results; the final draft of the Transcontinental Treaty of 1819, for example, is not printed as its important sections are available in other books, but Adams' personal views which shaped that crucial pact are given in some detail. Several of the more important documents in this respect, notably the July 4, 1821, address and the speech of 1841 on the Opium War, are not easily available in other editions. It has been the man who made history, not the documents which reflect the results, with which I have been primarily concerned in this book.

# CONTENTS

John Quincy Adams and
American Continental Empire

# JOHN QUINCY ADAMS
## *AN INTRODUCTION*

John Quincy Adams continues to rank as the greatest Secretary of State in American History. His accomplishments during the 1814 to 1828 era mark that decade and a half as the Golden Age of American diplomacy. In those years the United States signed the peace treaty which concluded the War of 1812, issued the Monroe Doctrine, and strengthened its maritime power through an agreement with England to clear the Great Lakes of warships and by obtaining rights to fish the rich banks of Labrador and Newfoundland. Americans extended their landed empire through the annexation of Florida, by removing Russian influence from the southwestern coast of the North American continent, through the establishment of the American-Canadian boundary from the Great Lakes to the Rockies, and, perhaps most important, by staking their first claims to the Pacific Coast. Adams participated in all of these events; in most he was the central figure. His story is the story of many of American diplomacy's finest hours.

Adams, however, not only extended American power; he also attempted to consolidate it. Much of his public service, especially his term in the Executive Mansion, was devoted to a tragically unsuccessful attempt to prevent the disintegration of the Union. Few nations in history have lacked men willing to conquer; but few nations have produced states-

men who successfully preserved and assimilated the areas con-
quered. Adams attempted to reach this pinnacle of statesman-
ship, and although he failed, he remains an heroic and tragic
figure whose failures are as instructive as his triumphs.

Adams' heritage, early experience, and education uniquely
prepared him for his career. No American statesman has enjoyed such an apprenticeship in international affairs as young
John Quincy, and only a few—Washington and Lincoln come
to mind—were as well prepared to understand the Union they
served. Born in Braintree, now Quincy, Massachusetts, on
July 11, 1767, John Quincy was the son of John and Abigail
Adams. The father, a guiding force in the triumph of the
American Revolution, later served as the new nation's second
President. Until his death on July 4, 1826, during his son's
presidential term, he was John Quincy's exemplar and
counselor.

Abigail, one of the brilliant women of her time, molded
her son's conscience. The younger Adams ultimately moved
away from the Calvinist rituals of his youth and became a
Unitarian, but he never sought escape from Abigail's stern
moral principles. "Adhere to those religious sentiments and
principles which are instilled into your mind," she wrote her
eleven-year-old son, then bound for France with his father's
diplomatic mission, "and remember that you are accountable
to your Maker for all your words and actions." The many
references to morality and religious faith which appear in her
son's writings may at times sound stilted, but they emanated
from a soul that premised its existence and all of its acts on
the presence of a Divine Will which had created an immutable moral order.

This faith largely explains Adams' view of the Union.
He believed that Providence had created the United States
to civilize the North American continent and, through ex-

ample, to eradicate from the face of the earth all forms of European colonialism. His experiences during the American Revolution confirmed this faith. Holding his mother's hand, he witnessed the bloodshed of Bunker's Hill, and as a youthful traveling companion of his father, he saw first-hand the brutal diplomatic struggles which consummated the American victory.

To these two beliefs, his confidence that the American Union held a pre-eminent place in God's moral order and his appreciation of the Revolutionary struggles, a third element was added to form the bedrock of his diplomatic and political philosophy. Knowledge, Adams constantly preached, is power. Young John Quincy used calculus, quoted the original Latin and Greek classics, studied contemporary European and American literature, constantly refreshed his unparalleled knowledge of international law, utilized six languages, and while not yet twenty discussed political theory and contemporary events with the leading men of Europe and America. In his classic report on weights and measures, published in 1821, Adams employed such a high level of mathematics and scientific knowledge that few of his contemporaries could follow his evidence and reasoning. He led the drive for the establishment of American astronomical observatories and was the pivotal figure in the creation of the Smithsonian Institution in Washington, D.C.

Adams did not spend all of his time thinking Great Thoughts, however. That he had to renounce expressly the attraction which actresses held for him, a feat he performed in one of his more interesting and revealing letters, hints of some personal traits other than will power. He achieved some fame in the better social circles as a wine-taster, a skill which demands practice. Many gay occasions at both European and American theaters found Adams in attendance, and his

letters include some pungent drama criticism. He loved to
exercise. Washingtonians often sighted the Secretary of State,
later the President, floating or swimming down the Potomac.
He usually wore only a skullcap and goggles. During the
winter he walked regularly from the White House to Capitol
Hill and back. The speed with which he usually traveled this
distance must remain a record, at least for men old enough
to be President.

These diversions, however, never distracted him from the
main objective of his life: to use his knowledge, education
and faith to extend and to strengthen the Union. Before he
reached his twenty-eighth birthday his abilities had attracted
the attention of George Washington, who sent Adams as
American Minister-Resident to the Netherlands in 1794-1795.
The following year many of Adams' private political views
became American dogma when Washington published his
Farewell Address, although John Quincy had no direct influence in formulating this state paper. In 1797 Adams became American Minister-Resident in Prussia, returning home
shortly after Thomas Jefferson defeated John Adams in the
1800 campaign.

Contemporaries viewed the victory of the supposedly radical Jefferson as a dramatic shift in their nation's history, but
John Quincy's career soon provided contrary and more reliable
evidence. Massachusetts Federalists elected him to the Senate
in 1802, and for the next six years the son of the Federalist
second President moved step by step with the foreign policies,
and many of the domestic measures, of the new administration. Adams was the only Federalist in the Senate who
approved Jefferson's purchase of the Louisiana territory,
although he believed that American government could be
extended over the newly purchased territory only by a
constitutional amendment; other Federalists feared that the

acquisition would either drain New England of its political power or lead to the break-up of the Union.

During these years Adams formed a close friendship with Secretary of State James Madison, whose immense intellectual capacities and belief in an expansive, cohesive system closely resembled Adams'. And the young Massachusetts Senator did not hesitate to vote for Jefferson's and Madison's far-reaching Embargo measure of 1807-1808, a weapon which the administration hoped would force England and France, then locked in the Napoleonic struggles, to recognize the American claim of the right to almost unrestricted trade with both belligerents. The Embargo might have been in the national interest and it perhaps protected American property from the two European giants, but it also allowed grass to grow on the once-busy wharves of Boston and Salem. As a consequence, angry Massachusetts Federalists evicted Adams from the Senate in 1808. Newly elected President James Madison then re-employed his friend by appointing him American Minister to Russia, a post which Adams later recalled as an "honorable diplomatic exile" after his losing battle with the Federalists.

In supporting the Louisiana Purchase and the Embargo, Adams simply voted his life-long convictions. His enemies accurately characterized his passionate concern for both American commercial and landed expansion when they sarcastically described him as an amphibious animal—one who moved on both land and sea. His interest in maritime rights derived from his New England background and from his belief that America's prosperity depended in large measure upon the freedom enjoyed by American fishing fleets and commercial shipping. He jealously protected the fishing rights in Newfoundland and Labrador claimed by his father during the negotiations of 1783; the son's main attention at Ghent in 1814, when the second Anglo-American peace treaty evolved, riveted on the fisheries. John Quincy's gifted son, Charles Francis Adams, carried on this family duty when he once more preserved American fishing rights in the Treaty of London in 1871. The Adamses treasured these rights not only because the fisheries employed many Americans, but because they also brought in badly needed gold and silver coins when the catch was marketed in Europe. This specie helped enable the United States to pay its debts to Europe.

Adams explored every possibility for the expansion of American commerce, battling continually against any discrimination placed on his nation's goods or maritime rights. His weapons were the traditional American principles of reciprocity and freedom of the seas; his target was the colonial empires, especially those in the Western Hemisphere. During his first term in the State Department he spent considerable labor to enlarge American trading rights in the rich British West Indies. London finally surrendered some privileges in the spring of 1822. These, however, left the ambitious Adams dissatisfied, so he pushed for more with the surprising argument that the trade of the British empire should be open to Americans and British on much the same terms. Peeved British officials slammed the door shut once again, and the islands remained closed until the Jackson Administration reached a compromise with England in 1830. Adams also made several attempts to abolish privateering and to establish the rights of neutral shipping in time of war. This passion for commercial expansion partly explains both his hope of wielding the Monroe Doctrine to prevent British trading monopolies in Latin America, and his request as President that Congress send emissaries to the first inter-American meeting in Panama in 1826.

Adams had expressed these views long before President James Monroe appointed him Secretary of State in 1817. On his mission to St. Petersburg from 1809 until 1814 he found in Czar Alexander not only a personal friend but a powerful European figure who agreed that freedom of the seas was doubly desirable: the principle sounded correct morally and held the more immediate attraction of wounding the British commercial monopolies. Adams placed this last objective, the dismantling of the British Empire, and indeed of the whole of all European colonial empires, high on his list of diplomatic priorities. He interpreted the American Revolution as signaling the beginning of the end for the colonialists. In time, he believed, all of North America must fall into American hands. During the famous conversation with British Minister Stratford Canning in 1821, on possible British claims to the moon, Adams disavowed American claims to Canada. But one feels that this was similar to his disavowal of wishing to use force to take Cuba: neither force nor a hurried policy of aggrandizement was necessary, for Cuba and Canada would in due time fall into American hands like ripe apples. As the bellicose phrases of his July 4, 1821 address reveal, colonialism became an intensely moral and personal matter to him.

This anti-colonial crusade, of course, had the more positive fascination of extending United States empire in North America. Adams' great triumph, in this respect, was the Transcontinental Treaty of 1819; this pact, as Adams' biographer Samuel Flagg Bemis has written, stands as the most magnificent diplomatic victory ever achieved by a single American. Since colonial days, Adams' countrymen had coveted the Spanish-controlled Floridas. West Florida fell into American hands between 1810 and 1813 after a series of daring and rather disreputable raids approved by President Madison. In 1817 Adams opened negotiations with Luis de Onís, the smooth Spanish Minister to the United States, to obtain East Florida, or what is now the state of Florida. Complications immediately arose. Spain demanded that the United States surrender any claims to Texas which might have been obtained in the Louisiana Purchase. These claims were shadowy, but Adams was nevertheless reluctant to surrender them. He did so only after the Monroe Cabinet instructed him to acquiesce. Spain also demanded that the United States promise not to recognize the revolutionary nations of Latin America which claimed their independence from Spain. Again Adams balked; he refused to tie his hands before dealing with such a vital question as the Latin American revolutions. This time the Cabinet supported him. Adams countered with the demand that Spain surrender her claims to the Northwest Pacific coast to the United States; this would give Americans their first foothold on the Pacific. Onís was ready to meet this request. but the talks deadlocked on the recognition issue.

In late 1817, however, the negotiations were jolted when General Andrew Jackson, ordered by Monroe to end Indian forays across the Florida border, pursued the Indians into Florida, seized several Spanish towns, and hanged two British adventurers who had been aiding the Indians. Of the five Cabinet members only Adams argued to support Jackson and to use the raid as a lever to force Spain to sell Florida. The Secretary of State won his point, and Spain, faced with such direct evidence of her crumbling power in Florida, surrendered the area and also her claims to the Pacific coast.

Adams' shrewdness in dealing with Onís, his audacity in supporting Jackson, and his foresight in demanding the claims on the Northwest coast, are unsurpassed in American diplomatic annals. His deserved exaltation over this triumph, however, was short-lived. The Spanish government stalled its ratification of the agreement in the hope that Adams would not recognize the rebellious colonies. Spain finally ratified in 1821, and a year later the United States began extending formal diplomatic recognition to the new nations.

Then a more ominous danger loomed. Several of the European powers, principally France and Russia, began to lay plans for planting new colonial empires in the New World. Perhaps France posed the gravest danger. Throughout the spring and summer of 1823 she gained control of the Spanish throne and threatened to use troops to restore Latin America to Spanish, that is, French, rule. The more immediate peril to the United States, however, developed when Czar Alexander, Adams' one-time friend, issued a ukase in 1821 which struck at the growing New England trade in furs and metals with the Pacific Coast by excluding non-Russian ships within a one hundred mile distance of Russian possessions on the Northwest coast. The ukase also planted Russian territorial claims into the Oregon country, an area where British, Russian and American interests conflicted and which Adams now considered exclusively American.

Great Britain valued both her commercial ties with the new Latin American nations and her possessions in the Northwest. She consequently found common interest with the United States in opposing the French and Russian pretensions. In the summer of 1823 the British government offered to join the United States in announcing to France that Latin America was not to be molested. Monroe, John Calhoun, and former Presidents Jefferson and Madison wanted to grasp this offer; their case became stronger when in mid-November, 1823, the Czar informed Monroe that Russia hoped Latin America would be restored to Spanish rule. Adams, however, successfully urged that in spite of the threatening French and Russian moves the United States should, instead of appearing as England's junior partner, unilaterally issue its own declaration. Using his Secretary of State's analyses as the core of his message, Monroe announced his doctrine to the world on December 2, 1823. Faced with this American attitude, and, of more consequence, confronted with the power of the British fleet, the French trimmed their ambitions in the New World. Adams meanwhile dealt with the Russians through direct, bilateral negotiations. Less than five months after the Monroe Doctrine became public, the Czar agreed to rescind the one hundred mile limit and also to move Russian territorial claims out of the Oregon country and north to 54° 40', now the southern border of Alaska.

The Czar's retreat left only conflicting British and American interests in the Northwest, but Adams had already stalled the British. In an agreement signed in 1818 and renewed in 1827, he rescued weak American claims in Oregon by winning a British pledge that the territory would be open to the citizens of both nations. American settlers and traders soon established a sizable beachhead. Under the prodding of President James K. Polk, who received vigorous encouragement from the seventy-nine-year-old Congressman Adams, the British surrendered the area between the Columbia River and the 49° parallel in 1846.

Adams must also be credited with a diplomatic triumph for the drawing of the United States-Canadian boundary between the Great Lakes and the Rockies along the 49° parallel. Great Britain had hoped to have the line drawn one hundred and fifty miles further south in order to give British traders direct access to the Mississippi River. Adams' achievement not only prevented the British from enjoying this access, but also kept large sections of the future states of Minnesota, North Dakota, Montana, and, ultimately, Washington in American hands, and thus, unknowingly to be sure, also preserved the rich Mesabi iron ore range for the future American iron and steel empire.

As these actions indicate, and as Adams candidly confessed in his diary, he would not rest until Europeans accepted the United States and North America as one and the same.

He differed from most of his many fellow expansionists, however, on one crucial question: he harbored little ambition to
move American territorial claims beyond the continent. Adams
feared that too vast an expanse of land could become un-
manageable, particularly if large areas were non-contiguous.
This fear mounted during the inflamed Missouri Compromise
struggle of 1820 when he first fully glimpsed the menace
which the slavery debate held for the American empire.

The Secretary of State now began to change the emphases in
his imperial plans; the first important result of this reformu-
lation was his July 4 address of 1821. The following year he
cautioned against scheming Cuba away from Spain. A year
later Adams' continued insistence convinced Monroe to drop
the warnings from his 1823 message that the United States
might directly interfere to help revolutionaries in Greece. His
diary entry of March 9, 1821, recording the conversation with
Henry Clay, illustrates Adams' desire to keep American hands
off the Latin American revolutions. He finally agreed in 1822
to Monroe's and Clay's continual pleas for recognition, but
his instructions to the initial American ministers to the new
Latin American nations are extremely cautious in discussing
political questions.

Ambiguities and contradictions abounded in these acts.
Adams wanted ultimately to annex Cuba, yet warned against
annexation; he opposed political entanglements with Latin
America in 1821-1822, but hovered on the brink of such
involvements in 1826; and he deprecated colonial empires,
yet refused to use American power to weaken those empires
except in North America, and even then used power selec-
tivly and most cautiously. Some of these dilemmas were more
apparent than real; in the last-mentioned case, for example,
Adams constantly feared that his nation's intervention in
foreign wars would soon destroy American liberties. Not even

an anti-colonial war was worth that price. At several crucial junctures, however, Adams found himself confronted with a cruel paradox: the fulfillment of his fervent belief in the ordained expansion of the American people would, in some instances, enlarge the area of slavery and, in most cases, accelerate the ripping of the seams of Union.

His inability to escape this entrapment finally led Adams to brand his whole life a failure, but he rendered this verdict only after a desperate attempt to work out a radical solution. He began by affirming that the United States had a utopia to perfect internally, not externally. Union and liberty, Adams preached, begins at home, not abroad. In the context of this belief he advocated a nationally planned and financed system of internal improvements which would fasten together all sections of the Union with strands of railroads, canals and roads. Such a scheme would particularly enable the South to participate with the burgeoning Northeast in the exploitation of the West. Borrowing these ideas partly from Washington and Gallatin, but formulating the plan mostly from observations he had made as early as the 1790's, Adams trusted that this vision could be realized through the proceeds derived from the sale of the public lands.

The plan became not Adams' greatest legacy to his country, as he had hoped, but the cause of his political downfall, for he urged it at precisely that point in American history when Westerners, rapidly gaining strength under the Jacksonian banner, demanded free land, and when Southern and Western politicians, led by Calhoun, urged comprehensive state-rights. Consequently when Adams announced his plan in 1825 in his first annual message as President, he was jeered throughout much of the country. His support continued to dwindle because of his inept use of presidential power. He lacked the personal warmth that wins the hearts of voters, and his adherence to principle alienated many of his professional political supporters as well. When Adams did attempt intrigue he blundered, and for one particular misstep he paid dearly. No candidate won a majority of the electoral votes in 1824; Jackson had garnered the highest number with Adams and Clay trailing. When the House of Representatives met to select the Executive, Clay threw his support behind Adams who then was able to defeat Jackson. Shortly after, the President-elect named Clay Secretary of State. Jacksonians screamed their protests and promised suitable revenge for such a deal, a pledge they later fulfilled. No explicit evidence has appeared of an understanding between Adams and Clay, but doubtless the two men fully understood each other and both comprehended the ingredients necessary in 1824 for the making of the President and the Secretary of State.

Adams never overcame the opposition aroused by this arrangement with Clay, and the immediate weakening of his political power dealt a fatal blow to his internal improvements plan. By 1826 Adams believed he had no chance for re-election. The voters proved this to be accurate prophecy in 1828. After remaining out of national politics for two years he returned in 1831 as Congressman from his home district in Massachusetts, the only retired President who has re-entered politics through election to national office. He held this victory a high honor and won continual re-election until his death seventeen years later.

These were memorable years. Adams became the foremost spokesman in Congress against slavery, winning the nickname of "Old Man Eloquent" for his reasoned, moralistic attacks on the Peculiar Institution. He led the onslaught against the gag rule which had been imposed by Congress in an effort to stop the flood of anti-slave petitions from New England

and the Midwest. Adams attacked this rule so viciously that in 1842 Southerners attempted to censure his actions. The seventy-five-year-old man answered with an impassioned speech which forced his opponents to withdraw the censure motion. Two years later the House repealed the gag rule.

Adams was not as successful in his final crusade. He bitterly assailed President James K. Polk's attempt to declare war on Mexico in 1846. Adams despised the ensuing conflict not only because of its odious origins—many Americans, including Abraham Lincoln, then a young colleague of Adams in Congress, believed that Polk had forced the war on Mexico in order to seize California and New Mexico—Adams also attacked Polk's declaration because it opened the floodgates of expansion and raised in its most virulent form the slavery issue. The old man did not oppose all expansion. He fought, for example, to annex the Oregon territory at this time. But Adams interpreted the war as an attempt by Polk to move beyond proper continental limits through the use of force and, even more abominable to Adams' mind, to expand the area of slavery. He steadily opposed Polk's course throughout 1847 and early 1848. Then, on February 21, 1848, a resolution reached the House floor which proposed awarding medals to American army officers fighting in Mexico. Adams firmly cast a vote of "No." Seconds later he slumped unconscious into his seat. Two days after this final protest against a war which was to make real his old, impassioned dreams of American continental empire, John Quincy Adams died at the age of eighty years and seven months.

# CHAPTER I

# THE MAN

Adams studied science, theater, and religion much as he studied international affairs. In his many-faceted personality, however, two characteristics repeatedly appear: the concern for moral order and a regard for the community of men. In the first selection Adams starkly outlines his thoughts on these principles. His view of these and of the theater, self-discipline, science, and human nature follow. The comments on Henry Clay in the final selection reveal the characteristics of Adams as much as they do of Clay.

## 1. THE OBLIGATIONS OF AMERICAN STATESMEN
[To James Lloyd, October 1, 1822, *The Writings of John Quincy Adams*, VII, 311-313]

. . . The future capabilities of our country to constitute a power such as associated man has never yet exhibited upon earth are a never failing source of delight to the traveller who, in passing over any part of our almost boundless territory, carries with him a benevolent feeling and a reflecting mind. Our improvements of physical nature upon this continent seem to realize the enchantments of a fairy tale. Would it not be flattering ourselves too much to believe that our improvements in the condition of our moral existence are advancing with equally gigantic strides? Our constitutions of civil government so far as their character has been hitherto tested by experience are certainly very great improvements upon all the forms of polity that had before been established among men. The sparing delegation and cautious distribution of the power possessed by one man over the will and actions of another (with the exception of slavery), the very limited extent allowed to authoritative control, and the securities and hedges with which personal civil, political and religious liberty are surrounded, have conferred upon us advantages never before enjoyed by human beings. Individual liberty is individual power, and as the power of a community is a mass compounded of individual powers, the nation which enjoys the most freedom must necessarily be in proportion to its numbers the most powerful nation. But our *distribution* of the powers of government is yet imperfect, and although our complicated machine of two co-ordinate sovereignties has not yet fallen to pieces by its own weakness, it exists in perpetual jeopardy, and has already been many times kept together, not by the natural operation of the machine itself, but sometimes by the cement of national union stronger than all the conflicting authorities, and sometimes by those makers and breakers of all human purposes—Time and Chance. Upon these at least it is not wise to place much reliance. We have not succeeded in providing as well for the protection of property as of personal liberty. Our laws between debtor and creditor are inefficacious and secure justice to neither. Our banks are for the most part fraudulent bankrupts. Our judiciary is not independent in fact, though it is in theory; and according to the prevailing doctrine our *national* Government is constituted without the power of discharging the first *duty* of a nation, that of bettering its own condition by internal improvement. Our private morals are tarnished by the unexampled prevalence of drunkenness, and our popular elections and legislative assemblies, though I believe less corrupt than other bodies of the same description have ever been in Europe, are yet more infected with intrigue and trickery than beseems a virtuous republic. It is among the obligations of our statesmen to apply their ingenuity and exercise their influence for the corrections of these evils; to aim as far as their abilities extend towards the moral purification of their country from its besetting sins. First, by setting the example of private morality; and secondly, by promoting the cause in every way that they can lawfully act upon others. The more so as these are vices, excepting perhaps intemperance, of which we hear little in the pulpit and even in the schools.

But that I may not run into a sermon, let me thank you once more for the permission to give your letter to the public, and renew the assurance of the respect and long rooted attachment of your servant and classmate.

## 2. NEVER FORM AN ACQUAINTANCE WITH AN ACTRESS

[To Louisa Catherine Adams, August 28, 1822, *The Writings of John Quincy Adams,* VII, 298-299]

. . . You ask me why I frequent the theatre. First, because having paid for admission for two persons by my two shares it is the only interest I get for my money, and the tickets cost me nothing. Secondly, because I have all my life had a very extravagant fondness for that species of entertainment, and always indulge myself with it, unless when motives of prudence, or propriety, or pride, or duty of some kind real or imaginary, prescribe to me the self-denial of them. Perhaps this is news to you, after more than twenty-five years of marriage. It is nevertheless true. The stage has been to me a source of much amusement for more than forty years. But I have always enjoyed it with discretion; first, with reference to expense, but secondly and chiefly, with respect to morals. To which end I have made it a rule to make no acquaintance with *actresses*. The first woman I ever loved was an actress, but I never spoke to her, and I think I never saw her off the stage. She belonged to a company of children who performed at the Bois de Boulogne near Passy, when I lived there with Dr. Franklin [Benjamin Franklin] and my father. She remains upon my memory as the most lovely and delightful actress that I ever saw; but I have not seen her since I was fourteen. She was then about the same age. Of all the ungratified longings that I ever suffered, that of being acquainted with her, merely to tell her how much I adored her, was the most intense. I was tortured with the desire for nearly two years, but never had the wit to compass it. I used to dream of her for at least seven years after. But how many times I have since blessed my stars and my stupidity that I never did get the opportunity of making my declaration. I learnt from her that lesson of never forming an acquaintance with an actress to which I have since invariably adhered, and which I would lay as an injunction upon all my sons. But thirdly, my reason for going to the theatre now is that as yet I can do nothing else with the evening. This reason will soon cease. We have had Booth. We now have a man by the name of Wilson, and next week we are to have Cooper, all tragedy heroes. But I prefer Jefferson to them all. The broader the farce, the more I enjoy it. But I expect before it is over I shall be abused for it in the newspapers.

## 3. SELF-CRITICISM AFTER DINING OUT
[*Memoirs of John Quincy Adams*, IV, 131-132]

Philadelphia, October 12, 1818. We dined and spent the evening at Mr. W. Jones's, the President of the Bank of the United States. . . . I was not satisfied with myself this day, having talked too much at dinner. I never take a large share in conversation without saying things which I afterwards wish were unsaid. Yet, in the estimation of others, I pass off on the whole better when I talk freely than when silent and reserved. This sometimes stimulates me to talk more than is wise or proper, and to give to the conversation of mixed companies a tone of discussion which becomes irksome and tedious. Nor can I always (I did not this day) altogether avoid a dogmatical and peremptory tone and manner, always disgusting, and especially offensive in persons to whose age or situation others consider some deference due.


## 4. ON SCIENCE AND THE INFINITE
[*Memoirs of John Quincy Adams*, X, 38-39]

November 8, 1838. I read Pearson, S. 48, on the reading microscope; 49, on the plumb-line; 50, on the spirit-level; and 51, on artificial horizons. These are all inventions for improving and perfecting the great instrument of astronomical observation, the telescope. The practical usefulness of this science seems confined to navigators on the ocean, and they generally know little more of it than to take the altitude of the sun upon the meridian, and, with the help of tables in the Nautical Almanac, to work out their longitude. To me, the observation of the sun, moon, and stars has been for a great portion of my life a pleasure of gratified curiosity, of ever-

tion impatient. He has long since marked me as the principal rival in his way, and has taken no more pains to disguise his hostility than was necessary for decorum and to avoid shocking the public opinion. His future fortune, and mine, are in wiser hands than ours; I have never, even defensively, repelled his attacks. Clay has large and liberal views of public affairs, and that sort of generosity which attaches individuals to his person. As President of the Union, his administration would be a perpetual succession of intrigue and management with the legislature. It would also be sectional in its spirit, and sacrifice all other interests to those of the Western country and the slave-holders. But his principles relative to internal improvements would produce results honorable and useful to the nation.

# CHAPTER II

# THE CONCEPT OF EMPIRE

A North American continental empire under United States control comprised the polestar of Adams' diplomatic objectives. He envisioned this empire as founded upon and deriving its strength from individual liberty. The first selection in this chapter is his most memorable statement of this policy; the last sentence, when considered in the setting of 1819, is remarkable for its scope, simplicity, and lack of doubt. When President Monroe once questioned the long-term viability of a continental empire, Adams and John Calhoun of South Carolina, then Secretary of War in the Monroe Cabinet, quickly corrected the President's view.

Monroe's fears, however, were necessarily speculative, for his nation did not yet possess the western areas of the continent. British territorial claims particularly frustrated Adams' ambitions in the Northwest, as noted in the fine exchange between the Secretary of State and British Minister Stratford Canning. Six months after this encounter, Adams most strikingly elaborated his views on the British Empire in particular and colonialism in general in his July 4 address of 1821. The sarcasm he wielded in this speech is entertaining but somewhat unfortunate, for it tends to obscure the long and instructive paragraph on American ideals.

## 1. NORTH AMERICA WILL BE THE UNITED STATES

[*Memoirs of John Quincy Adams,* IV, 437-439]

November 16, 1819. At noon, after a mere call at the office, I attended at the President's, where Mr. Crawford [William H. Crawford of Georgia, Secretary of the Treasury] and Mr. Wirt [William Wirt of Maryland, Attorney General] soon afterwards came. . . .

[Crawford] said he had been conversing with Mr. Lowndes [William Lowndes, Congressman from South Carolina], who told him that, both in England and France, everybody with whom he had conversed appeared to be profoundly impressed with the idea that we were an ambitious and encroaching people, and he thought we ought to be very guarded and moderate in our policy, to remove this impression.

I said I doubted whether we ought to give ourselves any concern about it. Great Britain, after vilifying us twenty years as a mean, low-minded, peddling nation, having no generous ambitions and no God but gold, had now changed her tone, and was endeavoring to alarm the world at the gigantic grasp of our ambition. Spain was doing the same; and Europe, who, even since the commencement of our Government under the present Constitution, had seen those nations intriguing with the Indians and negotiating to bound us by the Ohio, had first been startled by our acquisition of Louisiana, and now by our pretension to extend to the South Sea, and readily gave credit to the envious and jealous clamor of Spain and England against our ambition. Nothing that we could say or do would remove this impression until the world shall be familiarized with the idea of considering our proper dominion to be the continent of North America. From the time when we became an independent people it was as much a law of nature that this should become our pretension as that the Mississippi should flow to the sea. Spain had possessions upon our southern and Great Britain upon our northern border. It was impossible that centuries should elapse without finding them annexed to the United States; not that any spirit of encroachment or ambition on our part renders it necessary, but because it is a physical, moral, and political absurdity that such fragments of territory, with sovereigns at fifteen hundred miles beyond sea, worthless and burdensome to their owners, should exist permanently contiguous to a great, powerful, enterprising, and rapidly growing nation. Most of the Spanish territory which had been in our neighborhood had already become our own by the most unexceptionable of all acquisitions—fair purchase for a valuable consideration. This rendered it still more unavoidable that the remainder of the continent should ultimately be ours. But it is very lately that we have distinctly seen this ourselves; very lately that we have avowed the pretension of extending to the South Sea; and until Europe shall find it a settled geographical element that the United States and North America are identical, any effort on our part to reason the world out of a belief that we are ambitious will have no other effect than to convince them that we add to our ambition hypocrisy.

## 2. DEBATE OVER THE POSSIBLE EXTENT OF EMPIRE

*[Memoirs of John Quincy Adams, VI, 250-251]*

March 9, 1824. There was, at one o'clock, a Cabinet meeting at the President's; Calhoun and Southard [Samuel Southard of New Jersey, Secretary of the Navy] present. It was principally to read the draft of a message to both Houses of

Congress, recommending the establishment of a military post high up the Missouri River, and another on the Pacific Ocean, at the mouth of the Columbia River or at the Straits of Juan de Fuca. But it was a strong argument against making any territorial settlement on the Pacific, with a decided expression of an opinion that they would necessarily soon separate from this Union. I suggested doubts of the expediency or necessity of communicating such an opinion.

Calhoun supported and enlarged upon my objections, and Southard concurred with us. The voice against the message was unanimous, and the President concluded not to send it.

Calhoun thought there would be no separation should we make settlements on the Pacific Ocean, and I inclined to the same opinion. He said the passion for aggrandizement was the law paramount of man in society, and that there was no example in history of the disruption of a nation from itself by voluntary separation.

I contested this, and cited the case of the tribes of Israel. He admitted this was an exception, but said it was the only one. The position was not correct. The separation of Portugal from Spain, and of Sweden from Denmark and Norway, might have been mentioned; but I did not press the discussion. We agreed in the result. I thought a Government by federation would be found practicable upon a territory as extensive as this continent, and that the tendency of our popular sentiments was increasingly towards union.

## 3. AMERICAN CONTINENTALISM, THE BRITISH EMPIRE, AND THE MOON

[*Memoirs of John Quincy Adams,* V, 250-253]

January 27, 1821. . . . There was in his [Stratford Canning, British Minister to the United States] manner an apparent effort of coolness, but no appearance of cheerfulness or good humor. . . .

He then took from his pocket the National Intelligencer of yesterday, folded down to the column in which the proceedings of the House of Representatives were reported, and, referring to the statement that Mr. Floyd [John Floyd of Virginia] had reported a bill for the occupation of the Columbia River, said that was an indication of intentions in this Government which he presumed would leave no question of the propriety of his application to me.

I told him it was precisely that in which its greatest impropriety consisted. . . .

"Sir," said I, "suppose Mr. Rush [Richard Rush, United States Minister to Great Britain] should be present at a debate in the House of Commons, and should hear a member in the course of a speech say something about the expediency of sending a regiment of troops to the Shetland Islands, or a new colony to New South Wales; suppose another member of Parliament should publish in a newspaper a letter recommending the same project; and suppose Mr. Rush should then go to Lord Castlereagh [British Foreign Secretary] and formally allege those two facts as his motives for demanding whether the British Government had any such intentions; and, if answered that very probably they might, he should assume an imperious and tragical tone of surprise and talk about a violation of treaties: how do you think it would be received?"

He said that *now* he fully understood me, and could account for what had passed; this answer was perfectly explicit. But did I consider the cases as parallel?

"So far as any question of right is concerned," said I, "perfectly parallel."

"Have you," said Mr. Canning, "any *claim* to the Shetland Islands or New South Wales?"

"Have you any *claim*," said I, "to the mouth of Columbia River?"

"Why, do you not *know*," replied he, "that we have a claim?"

"I do not *know*," said I, "what you claim nor what you do not claim. You claim India; you claim Africa; you claim —"

"Perhaps," said he, "a piece of the moon."

"No," said I; "I have not heard that you claim exclusively any part of the moon; but there is not a spot on *this* habitable globe that I could affirm you do not claim; and there is none which you may not claim with as much color of right as you can have to Columbia River or its mouth."

"And how far would you consider," said he, "this exclusion of right to extend?"

"To all the shores of the South Sea," said I. "We know of no right that you have there."

"Suppose," said he, "Great Britain should undertake to make a settlement there, would you object to it?"

"I have no doubt we should," said I.

"But, surely," said Mr. Canning, "proof was made at the negotiation of the Convention of October, 1818, of the claims of Great Britain, and their existence is recognized in it."

"There was no proof," I said, "made of any claim, nor, to my knowledge, any discussion of claim. The boundary to the Stony Mountains was defined; westward of them Great Britain had no settlement whatever. We had one at the mouth of the

Columbia, which, having been broken up during the war, was solemnly restored to us by the British Government, in fulfilment of a stipulation in the treaty of peace. We stipulated in the Convention that the ports and places on the Pacific Ocean should be open to both parties for ten years, and, taking all these transactions together, we certainly did suppose that the British Government had come to the conclusion that there would be neither policy nor profit in cavilling with us about territory on this North American continent."

"And in this," said he, "you include our northern provinces on this continent?" /

"No," said I; "there the boundary is marked, and we have no disposition to encroach upon it. Keep what is yours, but leave the rest of this continent to us."

"But," said he, "this affects the rights of Russia and of Spain."

"Russia and Spain," I replied, "are the guardians of their own rights. Have you, Mr. Canning, any right to speak in their name?"

"Why sir," said he, "I can assure you that Great Britain is in very close alliance with them."

"Yes, sir, Great Britain has strong allies; we know that very well," said I; "but they have not authorized you to speak for them."

"And do you wish me," said he, in a tone highly incensed, *"to report to my Government* what you have now said to me?"

"Sir," said I, "you may report to your Government just what you please. Report to them, if you think proper, every word that I have said to you, not only now, but at any time, or that I ever shall say, provided you report nothing but the truth, as I have no doubt you will."

He said he thanked me for the addition of that opinion. . . .

## 4. ADDRESS OF JULY 4, 1821

Fellow-Citizens:

Until within a few days preceding that which we have again assembled to commemorate, our Fathers, the people of this Union, had constituted a portion of the British nation; a nation renowned in Arts and Arms, who, from a small Island in the Atlantic Ocean, had extended their dominion over considerable parts of every quarter of the Globe. Governed themselves by a race of kings, whose title to sovereignty had originally been founded in *conquest,* spell-bound for a succession of ages under that portentous system of despotism and of superstition which in the name of the meek and humble Jesus had been spread over the Christian world, the history of this nation had, for a period of seven hundred years, from the days of the conquest till our own, exhibited a conflict almost continual, between the oppressions of power and the claims of right. In the theories of the Crown and the Mitre man had no rights. Neither the body nor the soul of the individual was his own. From the impenetrable gloom of this intellectual darkness, and the deep degradation of this servitude, the British nation had partially emerged. . . .

Fellow-Citizens, it was in the heat of this war of moral elements, which brought one Stuart to the block, and hurled another from his throne, that our forefathers sought refuge from its fury, in the then wilderness of this Western World.

They were willing exiles from a country dearer to them than life.—But they were the exiles of liberty and of conscience, dearer to them even than their country. . . .

Thus was a social compact formed upon the elementary principles of civil society, in which conquest and servitude had no part. The slough of brutal force was entirely cast off;

all was voluntary; all was unbiased consent; all was the agreement of soul with soul.

Other colonies were successively founded, and other charters granted, until, in the compass of a century and a half, thirteen distinct British Provinces peopled the Atlantic shores of the North American continent with two millions of freemen; possessing by their charters the rights of British Subjects, and nurtured by their position and education, in the more comprehensive and original doctrines of human rights. From their infancy they had been treated by the parent state with neglect, harshness, and injustice. Their charters had often been disregarded and violated; their commerce restricted and shackled; their interests wantonly or spitefully sacrificed; so that the hand of the parent had been scarcely ever felt, but in the alternate application of whips and scorpions. . . .

For the Independence of North America, there were ample and sufficient causes in the laws of moral and physical nature. The tie of colonial subjection, is compatible with the essential purposes of civil government, only when the condition of the subordinate state is from its weakness incompetent to its own protection. Is the greatest moral purpose of civil government the administration of justice? And if justice has been truly defined as the constant and perpetual will of securing to every one his *right,* how absurd and impracticable is that form of polity, in which the dispenser of justice is in one quarter of the globe, and he to whom justice is to be dispensed is in another; where "moons revolve and oceans roll between the order and its execution"; where time and space must be annihilated to secure to every one his right. . . . Are the essential purposes of civil government, to administer to the wants, and to fortify the infirmities of solitary man? To unite the sinews of numberless arms, and combine the councils of multitudes of minds, for the promotion of the well-being of all? The first moral element then of this composition is sympathy between the members of which it consists; the second is sympathy between the giver and the receiver of the Law. . . .

It is not, let me repeat, fellow-citizens, it is not the long enumeration of intolerable wrongs concentrated in this Declaration; it is not the melancholy catalogue of alternate oppression and entreaty, of reciprocated indignity and remonstrance, upon which, in the celebration of this anniversary, your memory delights to dwell. . . .

The interest, which in this paper has survived the occasion upon which it was issued; the interest which is of every age and every clime; the interest which quickens with the lapse of years, spreads as it grows old, and brightens as it recedes, is in the principles which it proclaims. It was the first solemn declaration by a nation of the only *legitimate* foundation of civil government. It was the cornerstone of a new fabric, destined to cover the surface of the globe. It demolished at a stroke the lawfulness of all governments founded upon conquest. It swept away all the rubbish of accumulated centuries of servitude. . . .

And now, friends and countrymen, if the wise and learned philosophers of the elder world; the first observers of nutation and aberration, the discoverers of maddening ether and invisible planets, the inventors of Congreve rockets and Shrapnel shells, should find their hearts disposed to enquire what has America done for the benefit of mankind? Let our answer be this: America, with the same voice which spoke herself into existence as a nation, proclaimed to mankind the inextinguishable rights of human nature, and the only lawful foundations of government. America, in the assembly of nations, since her admission among them, has invariably, though often fruitlessly, held forth to them the hand of honest friendship, of equal freedom, of generous reciprocity. She has uniformly spoken among them, though often to heedless and often to disdainful ears, the language of equal liberty, of equal justice, and of equal rights. She has, in the lapse of nearly half a century, without a single exception, respected the independence of other nations while asserting and maintaining her own. She has abstained from interference in the concerns of others, even when conflict has been for principles to which she clings, as to the last vital drop that visits the heart. She has seen that probably for centuries to come, all the contests of that Aceldama the European world, will be contests of inveterate power, and emerging right. Wherever the standard of freedom and Independence has been or shall be unfurled, there will her heart, her benedictions and her prayers be. But she goes not abroad, in search of monsters to destroy. She is the well-wisher to the freedom and independence of all. She is the champion and vindicator only of her own. She will commend the general cause by the countenance of her voice, and the benignant sympathy of her example. She well knows that by once enlisting under other banners than her own, were they even the banners of foreign independence, she would involve herself beyond the power of extrication, in all the wars of interest and intrigue, of individual avarice, envy, and ambition, which assume the colors and usurp the standard of freedom. The fundamental maxims of her policy would insensibly change from *liberty* to *force*. . . . She might become the dictatress of the world. She would be no longer the ruler of her own spirit.

Stand forth, ye champions of Britannia, ruler of the waves! Stand forth, ye chivalrous knights of chartered liberties and the rotten borough! Enter the lists, ye boasters of *inventive* genius. Ye mighty masters of the palette and the brush! Ye improvers upon the sculpture of the Elgin marbles! Ye spawners of fustian romance and lascivious lyrics! Come and enquire what has America done for the benefit of mankind! In the half century which has elapsed since the Declaration of American Independence, what have *you* done for the benefit of mankind? . . .

[America's] glory is not *dominion*, but *liberty*. Her march is the march of the mind. She has a spear and a shield: but the motto upon her shield is, *Freedom, Independence, Peace*. This has been her Declaration: this has been, as far as her necessary intercourse with the rest of mankind would permit, her practice. . . .

# CHAPTER III

# RECIPROCITY AND
# THE SLAVE TRADE

Adams prized a continental empire for its maritime as well as for its territorial advantages. Gaining access to the Pacific Coast, particularly to the Columbia River, would provide easy access to the other half of the world for American traders. His desire to open Asian markets to all Westerners, and the manner in which he utilized his moral and religious fervor to realize this desire, are illustrated in the first selection in the chapter. This marked one of the rare occasions that Adams showered kind words on British imperialism. As Secretary of State he battled to open wide the British West Indies to American ships. The second selection indicates Adams' displeasure at the 1822 act of Parliament which closely regulated the West Indies trade. As a result of the American counterdiscriminations, outlined in Adams' instruction, the British completely closed the islands to Americans.

This son of Massachusetts mercantilism also attempted to enlarge maritime rights by proposing to the British a comprehensive plan of neutral and belligerent rights in wartime. It is significant that Adams considered this proposal as important as the principles of the Monroe Doctrine which were being shaped at the same time. Although this sweeping proposal had slight chance of British acceptance, the lessons of the War of 1812 and Adams' humanitarianism led to a formal offer which Britain rejected.

His humanitarianism, however, necessarily weakened when the issue of the slave trade arose. An Anglo-American convention to stop this trade through the search and seizure of ships on the high seas was finally written in 1824, but the green memories of the impressment issue between 1805 and 1812 forced the Senate to refuse ratification. Adams forcefully expressed American feelings on this issue in an instruction of 1818.

## 1. THE OPIUM WAR AND THE SANCTITY OF COMMERCIAL RECIPROCITY

*[Proceedings of the Massachusetts Historical Society,* XLII (October, 1909-June, 1910), 295-325]

The existing state of the relations between the kingdom of Great Britain . . . and the Empire of China, opens for discussion questions of deep interest to the whole human race; and of pre-eminent interest to the People of the North-American Union.

Great Britain and China are at War. . . .

The Law of Nations then by which the right and wrong of the present contest is to be tried, is as between the parties themselves the general and necessary Law of Nations; but as it may affect the other Christian Nations whose rights are involved in the issue, it is the Christian Law of Nations which must furnish the principles for discussion. It may be necessary to remember this distinction. . . .

If the state of Nature between men is a state of Peace,

and the pursuit of happiness is a natural right of man, it is the duty of men to contribute as much as is in their power to one another's happiness. This is most emphatically enjoined by the Christian precept to love your neighbour as yourself. Now there is no other way by which men can so much contribute to the comfort and well-being of one another as by commerce or mutual exchanges of equivalents. Commerce is then among the natural rights and duties of men. And if of individuals, still more of communities; for as by the law of Nature every man though he love his neighbour as himself, must provide for his own preservation and for that of his family, before he can minister to the wants of his neighbour, it follows that he can give in exchange to his neighbour only the excess of the fruit of his labour beyond that which is necessary for his and their subsistence. The exchange itself may indeed be of necessaries, and that leads to the division of labour, one of the greatest blessings of association; but that cannot be without commerce. . . .

But China, not being a Christian Nation, its inhabitants do not consider themselves bound by the Christian precept, to love their neighbour as themselves. The right of commercial intercourse with them reverts not to the execrable principle of Hobbes, that the state of Nature is a state of War, but to the Law of Nature independent of the precept of Christianity. By that Law, every one has a right to buy, but no one is obliged to sell. Commerce becomes altogether a matter of convention. The right of each party is only to propose, that of the other is to accept or refuse, and to his result he may be guided exclusively by the consideration of his own interest, without regard to the interests, the wishes, or the wants of his neighbour.

This is a churlish and unsocial system. . . .

The vital principle of commerce is reciprocity; and although in all cases of traffic, each party acts for himself and for the promotion of his own interest, the *duty* of each is to hold commercial intercourse with the other,—not from exclusive or paramount consideration of his own interest; but from a joint and equal moral consideration of the interests of both. . . .

The fundamental principle of the Chinese Empire is anticommercial. . . . It admits no obligation to hold commercial intercourse with others. It utterly denies the equality of other Nations with itself, and even their Independence. It holds itself to be the centre of the terraqueous globe, equal to the Heavenly host, and all other Nations with whom it has any relations, political or commercial, as outside tributary barbarians reverently submissive to the will of its despotic chief. . . .

It is time that this enormous outrage upon the rights of human nature, and upon the first principles of the Rights of Nations should cease. These principles of the Chinese Empire, too long connived at, and truckled to by the mightiest Christian nations of the civilized world, have at length been brought into conflict, with the principles and the power of the British Empire; and I cannot forbear to express the hope that Britain, after taking the lead in the abolition of the African Slave trade and of slavery; and of the still more degrading tribute to the barbary African Mahometans, will extend her liberating arm to the farthest bounds of Asia, and at the close of the present contest insist upon concluding the Peace on terms of perfect equality with the Chinese Empire, and that the future Commerce shall be carried on upon terms of equality and reciprocity. . . .

Which has the righteous *cause*? You have perhaps been surprised to hear me answer Britain. Britain has the righteous cause. But to prove it, I have been obliged to show that the opium question is not the cause of the war, and my demonstration is not yet complete. The cause of the war is the Kotow! the arrogant and insupportable pretension of China, that she will hold commercial intercourse with the rest of mankind, not upon terms of equal reciprocity, but upon the insulting and degrading forms of the relation between lord and vassal.

## 2. RECIPROCITY AND THE BRITISH WEST INDIES TRADE

[*American State Papers, Class I, Foreign Relations,* V, 511-518]

[Mr. Adams to Mr. Rush]
Washington, June 23, 1823.

Sir: I have the honor of inclosing herewith copies of the correspondence between the British minister residing here, Mr. Stratford Canning, and this Department, since the close of the last session of Congress, relating to the act of March 1, 1823, "to regulate the commercial intercourse between the United States and certain British colonial ports."

This act was intended as a corresponding measure on the part of the United States to the act of Parliament of June 24, 1822. On the 24th of August, 1822, immediately after this act of Parliament was received here, the President of the United States issued the proclamation, a copy of which was transmitted to you. . . .

That proclamation was issued in conformity with an act passed at the preceding session of Congress which had provided that, on satisfactory evidence being given to the President of the United States that *the ports* in the islands or colonies in *the West Indies* under the dominion of Great

Britain *had been opened* to the vessels of the United States, the President should be authorized to issue his proclamation declaring that the *ports of the United States* should thereafter *be open* to the vessels of Great Britain employed in the trade and intercourse between the United States and *such islands or colonies,* subject to such *reciprocal* rules and restrictions as the President might, by such proclamation, make and publish, anything in the laws entitled "An act concerning navigation" or an act entitled "An act supplementary to an act concerning navigation" to the contrary nothwithstanding.

. . . When the act of Congress passed (May 6, 1822), it was not known what colonial ports would be opened by the expected act of Parliament, nor under what rules and restrictions. It was therefore expressed in general and indefinite terms, looking to the opening of *the* ports in the British West Indies generally, and manifesting the disposition to meet the British Government forthwith in *any* plan for opening the ports to the navigation of both countries upon terms of *reciprocity,* the laws of both countries having at that time interdicted the trade between the United States and those colonies in the vessels of either nation. . . .

If the object of this act of Parliament [passed June 24, 1822] was to open the ports of the British colonies in the West Indies and in America to the vessels of the United States upon terms of *reciprocity,* it was not well adapted to its purpose.

In the 15th section it is declared to be the intention and meaning of the act that the privileges granted by it to foreign ships and vessels shall be confined to the ships and vessels of such countries only as give *the like privileges* to British ships and vessels in their ports in America and the West Indies; and the King is authorized to issue his order in council *prohibiting trade and intercourse* under the authority of the act, if it shall appear to him that *the privileges granted by this act* to foreign ships and vessels are not *allowed* to British vessels trading to and from any such country or island under the provisions of this act.

Now, what are the *privileges granted by this act* to the vessels of the United States? That they may bring *directly,* and not otherwise, from some port of the United States, to certain colonial ports named in the act of Parliament, *and none others,* certain articles of merchandise specifically named, *and none others.* That upon their arrival, of all the articles which they are permitted to bring, they shall pay enormous duties upon that portion which consists of the productions of the United States, consumable in the colonies themselves; and the only portion which in the results of the trade would be to the United States profitable export, and to one part of the colonies necessary import; and these duties are to be paid while the British vessels, enjoying *all the privileges granted by this act,* possess the additional and exclusive privilege of carrying to the same West India ports, directly or indirectly, the same articles thus heavily charged when coming from the United States, but free from all duty when carried from the colony in North America to the colony in the West Indies. . . .

The act of Congress [of March 1, 1823], therefore, opens the ports of the United States to British vessels from the colonial ports enumerated in the act of Parliament, but not upon the identical terms prescribed in it.

The restrictions of the act of Congress are counterparts not only to the restrictions of that particular act of Parliament, but to the others to which the American trade to the Colonies is subject, whether by colonial laws or by the navigation act of Charles II; and as some of those British restrictions were of a character which we could not meet by *specific* counterparts, we meet them by analogical restrictions productive of the same result. This was insisted on by our plenipotentiaries at the discussion during the negotiation of the convention of 1818, and Great Britain could not justly expect that discriminating surcharges, the reserved right of levying which we unequivocally refused to sanction with our consent as a *bargain,* we should be ready to accept as a dispensation of British law. For an enumerated list of ports, part only of which are opened by the act of Parliament, we open *all* our ports in return; for an enumerated and very scanty list of importable articles, we agreed to receive in return all the valuable exportable articles of all the opened British colonies; for a duty of ten per cent. import, and of four or five per cent. on exports, upon the *value of the articles* of the trade, we retain a foreign tonnage duty of ninety-four cents per ton on British vessels employed in the trade, and ten per cent. additional (not upon the value of the article, but upon the import duty otherwise charged upon it) upon the articles imported in them.

It is doubtful whether these countervailing restrictions on our part will prove sufficient to enable our vessels to pursue the trade in equal competition with the British. Still more doubtful whether, under the double system of restrictions, the trade itself can be pursued in a manner which will relieve the British West India colonies from the distress which was rapidly hurrying them to ruin under the preceding restrictions of the navigation act of Charles II. Surely the British Government must be aware that profit is the *sine qua non* of trade, and that if they load with enormous duties the articles indispensable to the existence of their colonies, those duties must be paid by the colonies themselves, or they will smother the trade itself. If the object of the act of Parliament was merely to balance the advantages of our proximity to the West Indies, their duties of import are at least five-fold too heavy; and as to the export duty, how could it possibly be paid upon articles to be brought into our market in competition with the like articles, partly of our own produce, and most largely from Cuba, St. Domingo, and other West India islands, where no export duty exists. The result must be, and has already proved to be, that our vessels admitted to the British colonial ports can take no return cargoes, and must come away in ballast. So that if they could sell their outward cargoes at a profit upon which the trade could *live,* it must be paid in *specie* by the colonists, leaving their staple commodities to rot upon their plantations, or to the old monopoly of the market at *home.* . . .

I have explicitly assured Mr. Canning that the proclamation of the President, authorized by the third section of the act of Congress of March 1, 1823, cannot be issued without a declaration pledging the faith of the British Government that, upon the vessels of the United States admitted into *all and every one* of the enumerated ports, and upon any goods, wares, or merchandise imported therein, in the said vessels, no other or higher duties of tonnage or impost, and no other charges of any kind, are levied or exacted than upon all British vessels, (including all vessels of the colonies themselves,) or upon the like goods, wares, or merchandise imported into the said colonial ports from *anywhere,* including Great Britain and the other British colonies themselves; and that, until such proof shall be given, British vessels and their cargoes coming from the colonies to the United States must continue to pay our foreign tonnage and ten per cent. additional impost duties. . . .

## 3. NEUTRAL RIGHTS IN TIME OF WAR

*[Memoirs of John Quincy Adams, VI, 164-165]*

July 28, 1823. I called at the President's with the draft of instructions to R. Rush, to accompany the project of a Convention to regulate neutral and belligerent rights in time of war. The President had suggested a single alteration in the draft of a Convention which I had sent him on Saturday.

Mr. Calhoun came in while I was reading to the President the draft of the instruction, and, after I had finished, started several doubts as to the propriety of proposing this project at all. He was confident it would not be accepted by Great Britain; and I have no expectation that it will at this time. But my object is to propose it to Russia and France, and to all the maritime powers of Europe, as well as to Great Britain. We discussed for some time its expediency. I appealed to the primitive policy of this country as exemplified in the first treaty with Prussia. I said the seed was then first sown, and had borne a single plant, which the fury of the revolutionary tempest had since swept away. I thought the present a moment eminently auspicious for sowing the same seed a second time, and, although I had no hope it would now take root in England, I had the most cheering confidence that it would ultimately bear a harvest of happiness to mankind and of glory to this Union.

Mr. Calhoun still suggested doubts, but no positive objections, and the President directed me to send the draft of the articles round to the members of the Administration, and to call a meeting of them for to-morrow at one. I was not surprised at Mr. Calhoun's doubts. My plan involves nothing less than a revolution in the laws of war—a great amelioration in the condition of man. Is it the dream of a visionary, or is it the great and practicable conception of a benefactor of mankind? I believe it the latter; and I believe this to be precisely the time for proposing it to the world. Should it even fail, it will be honorable to have proposed it. Founded on justice, humanity, and benevolence, it can in no event bear bitter fruits.

## 4. REJECTION OF BRITISH PROPOSALS TO STOP THE SLAVE TRADE

[*American State Papers, Class I, Foreign Relations*, V, 72-73]

[The Secretary of State to Messrs. Gallatin and Rush] Washington, November 2, 1818.

. . . The President desires that you would make known to the British Government his sensibility to the friendly spirit of confidence with which the treaties lately contracted by Great Britain with Spain, Portugal, and the Netherlands, and the legislative measures of Parliament founded upon them, have been communicated to this Government, and the invitation to the United States to join in the same or similar arrangements, has been given. He wishes you also to give the strongest assurances that the solicitude of the United States for the accomplishment of the common object, the total and final abolition of that odious traffic, continues with all the earnestness which has so long and so steadily distinguished the course of their policy in relation to it. As an evidence of this earnestness, he requests you to communicate to them a copy of the act of Congress of the last session, in addition to the act of 1807, to prohibit the importation of slaves into the United States . . . and to declare the readiness of this Government, within their constitutional powers, to adopt any further measures which experience may prove to be necessary for the purpose of obtaining so desirable an end.

But you will observe that, in examining the provisions of the treaties communicated by Lord Castlereagh, all their essential articles appear to be of a character not adaptable to the institutions or to the circumstances of the United States.

The power agreed to be reciprocally given to the officers of the ships-of-war of either party to enter, search, capture, and carry into port for adjudication, the merchant vessels of the other, however qualified and restricted, is most essentially connected with the institution by each treaty of two mixed courts, one of which to reside in the external or colonial possessions of each of the two parties, respectively. This part of the system is indispensable to give it that character of reciprocity without which the right granted to the armed ships of one nation to search the merchant vessels of another would be rather a mark of vassalage than of independence. But to this part of the system the United States, having no colonies either on the coast of Africa or in the West Indies, cannot give effect.

You will add, that by the Constitution of the United States it is provided the judicial power of the United States shall be vested in a Supreme Court and in such inferior courts as the Congress may, from time to time, ordain and establish. It provides that the judges of these courts shall hold their offices during good behavior, and that they shall be removable by impeachment and conviction of crimes or misdemeanors. There may be some doubt whether the power of the Government of the United States is competent to institute a court for carrying into execution their penal statutes beyond the territories of the United States—a court consisting partly of foreign judges not amenable to impeachment for corruption, and deciding upon the statutes of the United States without appeal.

That the disposal of the negroes found on board the slave-trading vessels which might be condemned by the sentence of these mixed courts cannot be carried into effect by the United States; for if the slaves of a vessel condemned by the mixed court should be delivered over to the Government of the United States as freemen, they could not but by their own consent be employed as servants or free laborers. The condition of the blacks being in this Union regulated by the municipal laws of the separate States, the Government of the United States can neither guaranty their liberty in the States where they could only be received as slaves, nor control them in the States where they would be recognized as free.

That the admission of a right in the officers of foreign ships-of-war to enter and search the vessels of the United States in time of peace, under any circumstances whatever, would meet with universal repugnance in the public opinion of this country; that there would be no prospect of a ratification, by advice and consent of the Senate, to any stipulation of that nature; that the search by foreign officers, even in time of war, is so obnoxious to the feelings and recollections of this country, that nothing could reconcile them to the extension of it, however qualified or restricted, to a time of peace; and that it would be viewed in a still more aggravated light if, as in the treaty with the Netherlands, connected with a formal admission that even vessels under convoy of ships-of-war of their own nation should be liable to search by the ships-of-war of another.

You will therefore express the regret of the President that the stipulations in the treaties communicated by Lord Castlereagh are of a character to which the peculiar situation and institutions of the United States do not permit them to accede. The constitutional objection may be the more readily understood by the British cabinet if they are reminded that it was an obstacle proceeding from the same principle which prevented Great Britain from becoming, formally, a party to the Holy Alliance. . . .

# CHAPTER IV

# NEGOTIATING AT GHENT, 1814

In 1814 Adams left his diplomatic post in Russia and traveled across war-devastated Europe to join the American peace delegation at Ghent. Adams, Albert Gallatin, Henry Clay, James A. Bayard, and Jonathan Russell were stubborn and knowledgeable statesmen. The British delegation was less impressive. Partly because of this difference, the United States suffered few defeats in the negotiations despite notable reversals endured during the war.

The initial selection presents the terms which each nation first offered. The Americans blocked the creation of an Indian state and ultimately agreed to place the more important boundary disputes in the hands of commissions. The United States, however, failed to obtain British promises to halt the impressment of American sailors and to recognize American neutral rights on the high seas. These had been two of the leading causes of the war. Fortunately a long period of peace in Europe after 1814 enabled the British to discontinue these practices.

At times the greatest friction seemed to be not between the two delegations but within the American group and particularly between Adams and Clay. These arguments and their threatening implications are given in the second selection. Adams, following the statesman's principle of appealing to an opponent's self-interest, emphasized other issues when he advanced American claims to the fisheries in London in 1815. At this time he was American Minister to Great Britain. Both Adams and Clay finally won their points. In the Convention of 1818 the British were excluded from the Mississippi and the United States gained access to the banks of Newfoundland and Labrador.

The negotiations at Ghent did not produce unalloyed American successes. They fittingly introduced, however, the notable diplomatic triumphs of the following decade.

## 1. THE CONTEXT FOR NEGOTIATIONS

[*American State Papers, Class I, Foreign Relations,* III, 705-706]

[The American Peace Commission to James Monroe, Secretary of State]

August 12, 1814. We have the honor to inform you that the British commissioners, Lord Gambier, Henry Goulbourn, Esq. and William Adams, Esq. arrived in this city on Saturday evening, the sixth instant. . . . We accordingly met at one o'clock on Monday, the 8th instant. . . .

The British commissioners then stated the following subjects as those upon which it appeared to them that the discussions would be likely to turn, and on which they were instructed:

1st. The forcible seizure of mariners on board of merchant vessels, and, in connexion with it, the claim of His Britannic Majesty to the allegiance of all the native subjects of Great Britain.

We understood them to intimate that the British Government did not propose this point as one which they were particularly desirous of discussing; but that, as if it had occupied so prominent a place in the dispute between the two countries, it necessarily attracted notice, and was considered as a subject which would come under discussion.

2d. The Indian allies of Great Britain to be included in the pacification, and a definite boundary to be settled for their territory.

The British commissioners stated that an arrangement upon this point was a *sine qua non*. . . .

3d. A revision of the boundary line between the United States and the adjacent British colonies. . . .

After having stated these three points as subjects of discussion, the British commissioners added, that before they desired any answer from us, they felt it incumbent upon them to declare, that the British Government did not deny the right of the Americans to the fisheries generally, or in the open seas; but that the privileges formerly granted by treaty to the United States, of fishing within the limits of the British jurisdiction, and of landing and drying fish on the shores of the British territories, would not be renewed without an equivalent. . . .

There could be no hesitation on our part in informing the British commissioners that we were not instructed on the subjects of Indian pacification or boundary, and of fisheries; nor did it seem probable, although neither of these points had been stated with sufficient precision in the first verbal conference, that they could be admitted in any shape. We did not wish, however, to prejudge the result, or, by any hasty proceeding, abruptly to break off the negotiation. . . . We, therefore, thought it advisable to invite the British commissioners to a general conversation on all the points; stating to them, at the same time, our want of instructions on two of them, and holding out no expectation of the probability of our agreeing to any article respecting these.

At our meeting on the ensuing day, we informed the British commissioners that, upon the first and third points proposed by them, we were provided with instructions; and we presented as further subjects considered by our Government as suitable for discussion:

1st. A definition of blockade, and, as far as might be mutually agreed, of other neutral and belligerent rights.

2d. Claims of indemnity in certain cases of capture and seizure.

We then stated that the two subjects, 1st, of Indian pacification and boundary; 2d, of fisheries, were not embraced by our instructions. . . .

## 2. THE DISPUTE WITHIN THE AMERICAN DELEGATION

*[Memoirs of John Quincy Adams, III, 70-76]*

November 27, 1814. About eleven in the morning, Mr. Gallatin came into my chamber, with a note received from the British Plenipotentiaries. They have sent us back with this note the projet of a treaty which we had sent them, with marginal notes and alterations proposed by them. They have rejected all the articles we had proposed on impressment, blockade, indemnities, amnesty, and Indians. They have definitively abandoned the Indian boundary, the exclusive military possession of the Lakes, and the uti possidetis; but with a protestation that they will not be bound to adhere to these terms hereafter, if the peace should not be made now. . . . All the difficulties to the conclusion of a peace appear to be now so nearly removed, that my colleagues all considered it as certain. I think it myself probable. . . .

November 28, 1814. Mr. Gallatin's servant, Peter, brought me this morning, as the clock struck six, the British note and projet, with Mr. Gallatin's minutes upon them. . . . At eleven o'clock we met, and continued in session until past four. . . . [The British] have added a clause securing to them the navigation of the Mississippi, and access to it with their goods and merchandise through our territories.

To this part of the article Mr. Clay positively objected. Mr. Gallatin proposed to agree to it, proposing an article to secure our right of fishing and curing fish within the British jurisdiction. Mr. Clay lost his temper, as he generally does whenever this right of the British to navigate the Mississippi is discussed. He was utterly averse to admitting it as an equivalent for a stipulation securing the contested part of the fisheries. He said the more he heard of this the more convinced he was that it was of little or no value. He should be glad to get it if he could, but he was sure the British would not ultimately grant it. That the navigation of the Mississippi, on the other hand, was an object of immense importance, and he could see no sort of reason for granting it as an equivalent for the fisheries. Mr. Gallatin said that the fisheries were of great importance in the sentiment of the eastern section of the Union; that if we should sign a peace without securing them to the full extent in which they were enjoyed before the war, and especially if we should abandon any part of the territory, it would give a handle to the party there, now pushing for a separation from the Union and for a New England Confederacy. . . .

Mr. Clay said that there was no use in attempting to conciliate people who never would be conciliated; that it was too much the practice of our Government to sacrifice the interests of its best friends for those of its bitterest enemies; that there might be a party for separation at some future day in the Western States, too.

I observed to him that he was now speaking under the impulse of passion, and that on such occasions I would wish not to answer anything; that assuredly the Government would be reproached, and the greatest advantage would be taken by the party opposed to it, if any of the rights of the Eastern States should be sacrificed by the peace; that the loss of any part of the fisheries would be a subject of triumph and exultation, both to the enemy and to those among us who had been opposed to the war; . . . that as to the British right of navigating the Mississippi, I considered it as nothing, considered as a grant from us. It was secured to them by the Peace of 1783, they had enjoyed it at the commencement of the war, it had never been injurious in the slightest degree to our own people, and it appeared to me that the British claim to it was just and equitable. . . .

Mr. Clay said that by the British article now proposed they demanded not only the navigation of the river, but access to it through our territories generally, from any part of their dominions and by any road, and without any guard, even for the collection of our duties; that this might be an advantage to the people of Kentucky, for it was the shortest way to them for all imported merchandise. Goods could in that manner be sent by the St. Lawrence River from Europe to his house with a land carriage of not more than fourteen miles. But it would give the British access to our country in a dangerous and pernicious manner. It would give them the trade with the Indians in its full extent, and enable them to use all the influence over those savages which had already done us so much harm. . . .

November 29, 1814. . . . Mr. Gallatin brought us all to

unison again by a joke. He said he perceived that Mr. Adams cared nothing at all about the navigation of the Mississippi, and thought of nothing but the fisheries. Mr. Clay cared nothing at all about the fisheries, and thought of nothing but the Mississippi. The East was perfectly willing to sacrifice the West, and the West was equally ready to sacrifice the East. . . .

I then told Mr. Clay that I would make a coalition with him of the East and West. If the British would not give us the fisheries, I would join him in refusing to grant them the navigation of the river.

He said that the consequence of our making the offer would be that we should lose both.

## 3. THE IMPORTANCE OF THE FISHERIES

[*Memoirs of John Quincy Adams*, III, 265-269]

September 14, 1815. I went into London, and, as I had anticipated, found a note from Lord Bathurst appointing two o'clock this day to see me at Downing Street. . . .

I now stated the ground upon which the Government of the United States considered the right [to the fisheries] as subsisting and unimpaired. . . . These fisheries afforded the means of subsistence to multitudes of people who were destitute of any other. They also afforded the means of remittance to Great Britain in payment for articles of her manufacture exported to America. It was well understood to be the policy of Great Britain that no unnecessary encouragement or stimulus should be given to manufactures in the United States which would diminish the importations from those of Great Britain. But by depriving the fishermen of the United States of this source of subsistence, the result must be to throw them back upon the country and drive them to the resort of manufacturing for themselves, while, on the other hand, it would cut off the means of making remittances in payment for the manufactures of Great Britain. I might add that the people in America whose interests would be immediately and severely affected by this exclusion were in the part of the country which had always manifested of late years the most friendly dispositions towards Great Britain. This might perhaps be less proper for me to suggest than for a British Cabinet to consider. . . . I would say that fisheries, the nature of which was to multiply the means of subsistence to mankind, were usually considered by civilized nations as under a sort of special sanction. It was a common practice to leave them uninterrupted even in time of war. He knew, for instance, that the Dutch had been for centuries in the practice of fishing upon the coasts of this island, and that they were not interrupted in this occupation even in ordinary times of war. It was to be inferred from this that to interrupt a fishery which had been enjoyed for ages was itself an indication of more than ordinary animosity.

# CHAPTER V

# THE TRANSCONTINENTAL
# TREATY AND OREGON

The Monroe Administration's most spectacular diplomatic triumphs, the Transcontinental Treaty of 1819 and the Monroe Doctrine, resulted from a brilliant analysis by the Secretary of State of British, Russian, and Spanish ambitions and power in the New World. In the first selection Adams carefully assesses Russian and British influence in North America. This assessment proved vital when Adams moved to obtain the Floridas and frontage on the Pacific from Spain. The negotiations soon deadlocked, but General Andrew Jackson's foray into Florida revealed Spain's inability to control that area and gave Adams a trump card in the talks. When Jackson hanged two Englishmen who had incited the Indian attacks on American settlements, however, Spain hoped that England would intervene on behalf of the Spanish cause. But Great Britain refused to enter the dispute, partly because Adams issued two official notes which effectively presented to the world the American defense of Jackson's exploits. The first note, written by Monroe and Adams, is the third selection.

The accounts in Adam's diary of the course of the negotiations indicate many of the difficulties which he had to overcome to win this victory. He made only one serious misstep, the surrender of the weak American claims to Texas, and this was taken only after continued insistence by the other members of the Cabinet. The negotiations gave a magnificent display of Adams' diplomatic talents. He was fully entitled to linger over these events while recording his feelings in the diary.

After 1819, Adams devoted considerable attention to consolidating American claims in the Northwest. During the summer of 1823 he outlined the United States position to England and Russia. His manipulations of the suggested boundaries neatly played the two European powers against each other.

---

## 1. ASSESSING BRITISH AND RUSSIAN AMBITIONS IN THE WESTERN HEMISPHERE

[To George Washington Campbell, June 28, 1818, *The Writings of John Quincy Adams*, VI, 371-377]

. . . With regard to the views of Russia upon the northwest coast of this continent it is necessary to add only a few words to the instructions given to your predecessor. The Emperor Alexander, has never shown any symptoms of the passion which so vehemently prompted his ancestor Peter to make Russia a naval power; and in which the late Empress Catherine participated in so considerable a degree. The sale of line of battleships and frigates to Spain, is one proof among many, of his indifference to that instrument of power. The circumstances of the European world may have contributed to confirm him in this departure from the most remarkable and profoundest part of Peter's policy. The irresistible control over the north of Europe which he had acquired by the conquest of Finland and of Poland; the approximation in which they have brought him to the heart of Europe; and the ascendancy which, together with the late events, they have given him in all the European counsels, have probably taken such exclusive possession of his mind, that it has neither leisure nor inclination to occupy itself with the remote and contingent importance which can possibly be attached to the possession of a navy, in the future history of Russia. With the neglect of the navy, that of navigation and commercial shipping naturally follows; and without these, however the establishment of distant colonies may be attempted they can never flourish. It may be proper to observe attentively the movements of Russia with regard to their settlements on the north western coast; but they can never form a subject of serious difference, or jarring interest between that Empire and the United States. . . .

In the expectation that one or more of the three commissions appointed under the treaty of Ghent might eventuate in the disagreement of the commissioners, and that the recourse provided by the treaty on that contingency would become necessary, the minister of the United States in England has already been instructed to propose or to agree to the Emperor of Russia, as the sovereign to whom these appeals in the last resort should be submitted. Under these circumstances not only the views of the Russian government, with reference to their own settlements and pretensions on the north-west coast, acquire additional interest; but the whole system of Russian policy, as it bears on her relations with Great Britain, with the European alliance, with Spain and the South American affairs, may require the most steady and attentive observation, as it may link itself with objects of importance to the interests and welfare of the United States. . . .

The Emperor of Russia, who as the conservator of the peace

of Europe had already sided with Spain against the aggression of Portugal, seems now to have taken the same bias against the colonies, as the restorer of what he considered legitimate authority. Having no immediate interests of his own involved in the question, he appears to have viewed it only as a question of supremacy and obedience between the sovereign and his subjects, and to have taken it for granted that the sovereign must have the right, and the subjects the wrong of the cause. But Great Britain, the other efficient member of the alliance, had a great and powerful interest of her own to operate upon her consideration of the case. The revolution in South America had opened a new world to her commerce which the restoration of the Spanish colonial dominion would close against her. Her Cabinet therefore devised a middle term, a compromise between legitimacy and traffic; a project by which the political supremacy of Spain should be restored, but under which the Spanish colonies should enjoy commercial freedom, and intercourse with the rest of the world. She [England] admits all the pretensions of legitimacy until they come in contact with her own interest; and then she becomes the patroness of liberal principles and colonial emancipation. . . .

## 2. ADAMS, JACKSON, AND FLORIDA
[*Memoirs of John Quincy Adams,* IV, 107-115]

July 15, 1818. Attended the Cabinet meeting at the President's from noon till near five o'clock. The subject of deliberation was General Jackson's late transactions in Florida, particularly the taking of Pensacola. The President and all the members of the Cabinet, except myself, are of opinion that Jackson acted not only without, but against, his instructions; that he has committed war upon Spain, which cannot be justified, and in which, if not disavowed by the Administration, they will be abandoned by the country. My opinion is that there was no real, though an apparent, violation of his instructions; that his proceedings were justified by the necessity of the case, and by the misconduct of the Spanish commanding officers in Florida. The question is embarrassing and complicated, not only as involving that of an actual war with Spain, but that of the Executive power to authorize hostilities without a declaration of war by Congress. There is no doubt that *defensive* acts of hostility may be authorized by the Executive; but Jackson was authorized to cross the Spanish line in purusit of the Indian enemy. My argument is that the question of the constitutional authority of the Executive is precisely there; that all the rest, even to the order for taking the Fort of Barrancas by storm, was incidental, deriving its character from the object, which was not hostility to Spain, but the termination of the Indian war. This is the justification alleged by Jackson himself, but he also alleges that an imaginary line of the thirty-first degree of latitude could not afford protection to our frontiers while the Indians could have a safe refuge in Florida, and that all his operations were founded on that consideration. . . .

July 21, 1818. . . . The Administration were placed in a dilemma from which it is impossible for them to escape censure by some, and factious crimination by many. If they avow and approve Jackson's conduct, they incur the double responsibility of having commenced a war against Spain, and of warring in violation of the Constitution without the authority of Congress. If they disavow him, they must give offence to all his friends, encounter the shock of his popularity, and have the appearance of truckling to Spain. For all this I should be prepared. But the mischief of this determination lies deeper: 1. It is weakness, and a confession of weakness.

2. The disclaimer of power in the Executive is of dangerous example and of evil consequences. 3. There is injustice to the officer in disavowing him, when in principle he is strictly justifiable. These charges will be urged with great vehemence on one side, while those who would have censured the other course will not support or defend the Administration for taking this. I believe the other would have been a safer, as well as a bolder course.

## 3. JACKSON OFFICIALLY DEFENDED BY ADAMS

*[American State Papers, Class I, Foreign Relations,* IV, 497-499]

[The Secretary of State to Don Luis de Onís]
Washington, July 23, 1818.

I have had the honor of receiving your letters of the 24th June and 8th instant, complaining of the conduct of Major General Jackson in entering West Florida with the forces under his command, taking the Spanish posts of St. Mark and Pensacola, &c.

Without recurring to the long standing and heavy causes of complaint which the United States have had against Spain; to the forbearance with which they have been borne, without despairing of obtaining justice from her by amicable means; to the efforts equally unceasing and unavailing which they have made to obtain that justice; or to the extraordinary delays by which it has been protracted and is still withheld, it is thought proper on this occasion to call your attention to a series of events which necessitated and justified the entrance of the troops of the United States upon the Spanish boundary of Florida, and gave occasion to those transactions of the commander of the American forces against which you complain.

It cannot be unknown to you that, for a considerable time before the Government of the United States issued the orders for military operations in that quarter, the inhabitants of their frontier had been exposed to the depredations, murders, and massacres of a tribe of savages, a small part of which lived within the limits of the United States, far the greater number of them dwelling within the borders of Florida. The barbarous, unrelenting, and exterminating character of Indian hostilities is also well known to you. . . .

By the ordinary laws and usages of nations, the right of pursuing an enemy, who seeks refuge from actual conflict within a neutral territory, is incontestable. But, in this case, the territory of Florida was not even neutral. It was itself, as far as Indian savages possess territorial right, the territory of Indians, with whom the United States was at war. It was their place of abode; and Spain was bound by treaty to restrain them by force from committing hostilities against the United States—an engagement which the commanding officer of Spain in Florida had acknowledged himself unable to fulfill. Of the necessity there was for crossing the line, what stronger proofs could be adduced than that it was within that line that the American general met the principal resistance from the Indians which he encountered in the whole campaign; that within that line, at their towns which he destroyed, he found displayed, as barbarous trophies, the mutilated remnants of our wretched fellow-citizens, the murdered women and children, the accumulated barbarities of many years? . . .

The possession which [Jackson] took of the fort of St. Mark, and subsequently of Pensacola, was upon motives which he himself has explained, and upon his own responsibility. For his justification in the adoption of both those measures, he states them to have been necessary upon the immutable principles of self-defence:

That, at an early period of his operations, he had given full notice of their object to the Governor of Pensacola, by communication, dated the 25th of March last, warning him that every attempt on his part to succor the Indians, or prevent the passage of provisions for the American troops in the Escambia, would be viewed as acts of hostility:

That, in defiance of this admonition, the Governor of Pensacola did both give succor to the Indians, and delay the passage of the provisions to the American army, and thereby subjected them to the severest privations: . . .

A conduct not only so contrary to the express engagements of Spain, but so unequivocally hostile to the United States, justly authorizes them to call upon His Catholic Majesty for the punishment of those officers, who, the President is persuaded, have therein acted contrary to the express orders of their sovereign. . . .

In the mean time, I am instructed by the President to inform you that Pensacola will be restored to the possession of any person duly authorized on the part of Spain to receive it; that the fort of St. Mark, being in the heart of the Indian country, and remote from any Spanish settlement, can be surrendered only to a force sufficiently strong to hold it against the attack of the hostile Indians; upon the appearance of which force it will also be restored.

In communicating to you this decision, I am also directed to assure you that it has been made under the fullest conviction, which he trusts will be felt by your Government, that the preservation of peace between the two nations indispensably requires that henceforth the stipulations by Spain to restrain by force her Indians from all hostilities against the United States should be faithfully and effectually fulfilled.

## 4. NEGOTIATING THE TRANSCONTINENTAL TREATY

[*Memoirs of John Quincy Adams,* IV, 106-107, 218-221, 234-239, 253-267, 270]

July 10, 1818. Had an interview at the office with Hyde de Neuville, the French Minister—all upon our affairs with Spain. He says that Spain will cede the Floridas to the United States, and let the lands go for the indemnities due to our citizens, and he urged that we should take the Sabine for the western boundary, which I told him was impossible. He urged this subject very strenuously for more than an hour. As to Onís' note of invective against General Jackson, which I told him as a good friend to Onís he should advise him to take back, he said I need not answer it for a month or two, perhaps not at all, if in the meantime we could come to an arrangement of the other differences.

July 11, 1818. Mr. Onís, the Spanish Minister, called on me at my house to talk of the negotiation. He was more tractable upon the subject of Pensacola. . . . He then said they were willing to give us the Floridas for nothing, and, as there were large claims of indemnity for depredations on both sides, they were willing to set them off against each other, each of the two Governments undertaking to indemnify its own people. For all this they would only ask us to take the boundary westward at the Calcasieu or Mermentau, from the mouth to the source, thence a line to pass between Adeas and Natchitoches to the Red River, and from that to the

Missouri. I told him all the other points would now be easily adjusted but this last, which was impossible. . . .

January 15, 1819. Mr. Onís, the Spanish Minister, came by appointment at two, and I had further conversation with him upon the new instructions received by him from his Government. He says he is authorized to agree to a line from the Missouri to the mouth of the Columbia River, on the South Sea; that it was, at his earnest solicitation, agreed to in the Spanish Cabinet. He had written that it was essential to the completion of a great plan formed here of internal communication from the Atlantic to the Pacific Ocean, and that there was no prospect of our agreeing to any arrangement without it. . . . I told Onís that we could not agree to the proposal of drawing the line from the Missouri to Columbia River, but that if he would send me a written note his propositions would be considered. I said this because he himself seemed reluctant at writing unless we were ready to accept his offer. I therefore thought it best to make him write. . . .

January 29, 1819. I took my draft of a note to the Spanish Minister, Onís, to the President's. . . . The draft was approved with an alteration, and the letter was sent to him in the course of the day. It repeats the proposals made in my letter of 31st October, which were afterwards withdrawn, and requests Mr. Onís, if he has not power to accept either of them, to close the discussion, which must henceforth be useless. But the President directed me to see Mr. De Neuville and state to him that in consideration of the interest that his Government, and he personally, have taken in accomplishing an amicable arrangement of our affairs with Spain, I was authorized to say in confidence to him that we would agree to a modification of the western line proposed in my letter of 31st October, so as to avoid the difficulty objected against it, that it would pass within four or five leagues of Santa Fe. The offer is to take a line due north from the Pawnee bend of the Red River to the Arkansas, and follow the course of that to its source, in latitude forty-one, and thence by that parallel to the South Sea; but on condition that the Spaniards are to form no settlement north of the chain of Snowy Mountains. I accordingly sent to Mr. De Neuville, requesting him to call at the office this day. He came at four o'clock, and I stated to him this new proposal in confidence. He promised to see Onís and, without letting him know that we are prepared for this arrangement, ascertain whether he is prepared to agree to it. . . .

January 30, 1819. I received a note from the President, requesting me to attend at his house, and give notice to the other members of the Administration for a Cabinet meeting at one o'clock, to reconsider the offer confidentially made yesterday through the French Minister, Hyde de Neuville. . . . It was . . . unanimously approved, the four Secretaries and Attorney-General being present. On examining the map, however, it was discovered that I had made a mistake in the line yesterday proposed to be taken from the Red River north to the Arkansas, and that instead of the Pawnee bend, as I had understood, which is in longitude between ninety-six and ninety-seven, it was the bend in longitude one hundred and one. This accident affected and mortified me exceedingly. That in a transaction of such importance I should have been so inconsiderate and have taken so slight an inspection of the map as to have committed the mistake, was inexcusable to myself. . . .

On returning to the office, I sent immediately to De Neuville, requesting him to call at three o'clock. . . .

I began [the discussion with De Neuville] by rectifying the mistake I had made yesterday, which was done without difficulty, for, according to our agreement, he said he had spoken with Onís, not as having been authorized by me, but simply as of himself, and . . . had not even suggested to him the idea of asking for the line from the Pawnee bend, but had spoken of a range between longitude one hundred and two and ninety-eight. So that this difficulty was entirely removed. He then said that Mr. Onís had ample powers, which he had seen; that he had prepared a note to me, which I should receive this evening or tomorrow; that it would contain some further concession on the part of Spain, but the laboring point would be the line to the South Sea. Onís would now propose the southern branch of Columbia River, so that the line may yet terminate at its mouth. I told him that Spain having yielded the point of admitting us to the South Sea, it was impossible that she should have any interest in chaffering for four or five degrees of wilderness, which never will or can be of any value to her. To us they may be hereafter important, because the boundary for us will be not only with Spain, but with her successors. This he admitted. He said he would see me again, after I shall have received Onís's note.

February 1, 1819. Called upon the President, and had a conversation with him upon this renewal of negotiations with the Spanish Minister. There are various symptoms that if we do come to an arrangement there will be a large party in the country dissatisfied with our concessions from the Rio del Norte to the Sabine on the Gulf of Mexico. Clay has taken the alarm at hearing that Onís was again treating with us, and is already taking ground to censure the treaty, if one should be made. . . .

February 2, 1819. I called upon General Jackson, and mentioned in confidence to him the state of the negotiation with the Spanish Minister, and what we had offered him for the western boundary, and asked his opinion of it. He thought the friends of the Administration would be satisfied with it, but that their adversaries would censure it severely, and make occasion for opposition from it. He thought even that it would bring us again in collision with the Indians whom we are removing west of the Mississippi. . . . At the President's. I received from Mr. Onís a note yesterday proposing a line approaching considerably towards that which has been offered by us. I told the President of the letter signed "Franklin" which I have received, dated Lexington, Kentucky—of the preparation making, and sufficiently notified by Mr. Clay, to take ground against the western boundary offered by us to Spain, and what General Jackson had said to me. The President observed that while our differences with Spain should remain unadjusted, Mr. Clay would seize every incident arising from them to assail the Administration. If adjusted, he would use the adjustment itself for the same purpose. But the possession of the Floridas, with a clear and undisputed title, the acquisition of indemnity for the long-standing claims of our citizens upon Spain, and a recognized title extending to the South Sea, would be such advantages to this country, that he believed any opposition founded upon our consent to take the Sabine for the western boundary would have little weight with the people. . . .

February 12, 1819. I am so constantly occupied and absorbed by this negotiation with Onís that almost all other business runs in arrear, and in a most especial manner this journal. I rode to the President's, and the adjourned Cabinet meeting was held. The subjects left undecided yesterday were resumed, and I was finally authorized to accept the longitude one hundred from the Red River to the Arkansas, and the latitude forty-three to the South Sea, if better cannot be obtained. . . .

February 15, 1819. Mr. De Neuville, the French Minister, came and reported to me the substance of his interview with Mr. Onís relative to the counter-projet for a treaty which I sent to Onís the day before yesterday. He desired some further explanation with regard to my throwing into one the second article of his projet, and to the additional clause to it proposed by me. Without knowing what particular explanations were desired, I gave Mr. De Neuville the reasons for making one article of the two, and for the addition proposed. There were in this article, and in many others of the projet, sentimental professions of friendship and affection between the United States and the King of Spain, to say the least, entirely superfluous, and which I therefore struck out. But the boundaries of the Floridas, as his projet proposed to describe them, could not be admitted by us without giving up the ground for which we had always contended, that West Florida to the Perdido belonged to Louisiana. It was unnecessary for the contracting parties to say anything of their motives—unnecessary to say anything directly contrary to their past pretensions, and one of the most important principles in drawing up public compacts was brevity—as few words as possible to express with precision the agreement. . . .

A more formidable objection was made by Mr. Onís to my third article, containing the boundary line westward of the Mississippi. After a long and violent struggle, he had agreed to take longitude one hundred, from the Red River to the Arkansas, and latitude forty-two, from the source of the Arkansas to the South Sea. But he insisted upon having the middle of all the rivers for the boundary, and not, as I proposed, the western and southern banks; and he also insisted upon the free navigation of the rivers to be common to both nations. De Neuville urged these demands with great earnestness, and thought it was a point of honor which Onís could not abandon without humiliation.

I told him that I could see no humiliation in it. We were to agree upon a boundary, for which purpose the bank of a river was more simple and less liable to occasion future controversy than the middle of the river. It was extremely difficult to ascertain where the middle of a river throughout its course was. It would take a century to settle the middle of the Sabine, Red, and Arkansas Rivers, and to which of the parties every island in them would belong. . . . It was of no importance to Spain, who never would have any settlements on these rivers. But the United States would have extensive settlements upon them within a very few years. Then the islands in the rivers would be occupied, and questions of title and controversies with Spain [would arise]. My principle had been to cut up all this by the roots, which would be done by taking the banks of the rivers for the boundary. . . . De Neuville acknowledged that this view of the subject took away all ground of objection upon the point of honor, and said he would endeavor to convince Onís of it, but if the banks of the rivers were to form the boundaries, the Spanish settlers must at least have the use of the waters and the navigation of the rivers to the sea. I told him that such stipulation, if made, would be merely nominal, as there was not the remotest probability of there ever being any Spanish settlers there. I could not promise the acceptance of *any* variation from the projet I had now sent to Mr. Onís. . . .

Onís agrees to the tenth article, annulling the Convention of August, 1802. In the eleventh, he insists upon omitting the limitation of the sum to be assumed by the United States for payment of the claims of their citizens upon Spain to five millions of dollars. This was one of the points most strongly debated between us. I insisted that as this article particularly regarded the United States themselves, and we agreed to give a full discharge to Spain, she could have no right to ask the omission of the limitation, and if there should be no limitation of the sum, besides the uncertainty under which we should be, of what we should have engaged to perform, there would be great alarm here among the public, and exaggerated representations of the claims assumed, which might even endanger the ratification of the treaty by the Senate.

He said Onís was exceedingly anxious upon this article, and fearful that he would be blamed in Spain for having sold the Floridas for five millions of dollars. He said there were difficulties to get over in the King's Council at Madrid as well as in the Senate of the United States. There was an influence of priests in the Council, which was always counteracting the policy of the Ministers. . . .

I rejoined that it was notorious that the Floridas had always been a burden instead of a benefit to Spain; that, so far as her interest was concerned, to obtain five millions of dollars for them would be a bargain for Onís to boast of, instead of being ashamed—as a mere pecuniary bargain, it would be a hard one to us; that as to the priests, if Onís signed the treaty without transcending his powers, it would be too late when it should reach Madrid for them to resist its ratification—and he himself had told me that he had unlimited powers. . . .

February 18, 1819. Mr. Onís came to the office, and brought me a draft of the treaty in Spanish, as he said, according to the counter-projet offered by me, modified by the discussions which have taken place by the intervention of the French Minister, Mr. Hyde de Neuville. Onís himself has for the last ten days been confined to the house by chilblains, and this was the first time of his coming out. Upon reading over his projet, however, I found he had made some variations from the agreement as settled with De Neuville. He had in particular assumed the middle of the rivers for the boundaries, instead of the western bank of the Sabine and the southern bank of the Arkansas. I told him we should not agree to this

—when, to my astonishment, he told me that he had spoken of it last evening, at the drawing-room, to the President, who had promised him that we would agree to the middle of the rivers. I made no reply, but merely took it with the rest for reference. He importuned me again very obstinately to omit the limitation of five millions of dollars to the sum assumed by the United States to be paid to their citizens for claims upon Spain, and, finding me inflexible, he at last urged that at least we should agree to take six millions for the limitation—which, however, I still resisted. . . .

February 19, 1819. Cabinet meeting at the President's to consider the amended projet of a treaty with Spain, and the modifications still desired by Mr. Onís. . . . I remarked that Onís still insisted upon having the middle of the rivers; but I did not notice his assertion that the President at the drawing-room had promised him we would agree to it. I proposed that we should adhere to the principle of owning the rivers and all the islands in them ourselves, and of course to having the banks, and not the middle of the rivers, for boundaries. The President thought it was not a point upon which we should endanger the conclusion of the treaty. Mr. Thompson, Secretary of the Navy, asked if Onís would agree to take the banks of the rivers rather than break off. I said he would—he must; he had substantially agreed to it already. "Then," said Thompson, "insist upon it, by all means." The President acquiesced. . . .

February 20, 1819. Mr. Onís came this morning to my house, and told me that he must accept the treaty as now prepared, since we would have it so, though he still thought we ought to give up the limitation of the five millions, and the banks for the middle of the rivers as the boundaries. I observed there was no time left for further discussion, and we had yielded so much that he would have great cause to commend himself to his Court for what he had obtained. He said I was harder to deal with than the President, and he must say, as a suitor once said to Philip IV., " 'Sire, your Majesty has no influence with the Minister of Grace and Justice, for he refuses me what you have granted.' "


## 5. THE FAILURE TO OBTAIN TEXAS IN 1819
*[Memoirs of John Quincy Adams, V, 67-69]*

April 13, 1820. . . . Mr. David Trimble, a member of the House from Kentucky, called at the office. . . . His ostensible motive was to make up his opinion on the report to be made by the Committee of Ways and Means, of which he is a member. But he came with a long argument to convince me that the only way for me to make myself popular in the Western country was to set the treaty aside and urge the recognition of the South American revolutionists, and insist upon the Rio del Norte [the Rio Grande River] as the western boundary.

I told him that I understood the map of the country rather too well to suppose it would ever be possible for me to do anything that could make me popular in the Western country; that as to the treaty, I had never set the value upon it that was supposed, and of all the members of the Administration, I was the last who had consented to take the Sabine for our western boundary. I had no doubt that if the treaty should be set aside we should ultimately obtain more territory than it would secure to us, but we should get the same territory with the treaty sooner than we should want it; and even now I thought the greatest danger of this Union was in the overgrown extent of its territory, combining with the slavery question. I added as my belief, that there would be a majority of the House of Representatives now who would not accept of the province of Texas as a gift unless slavery should be excluded from it. Since the Missouri debate, I considered the continuance of the Union for any length of time as very precarious, and entertained serious doubts whether Louisiana and slavery would not ultimately break us up. . . .

As to the treaty, we could now very easily disengage ourselves from that. The difficulty would not be in setting it aside, but in obtaining it. He and Mr. Clay were excellent negotiators in theory. They were for obtaining all and granting nothing. They played a game between their own right and left hands, and could allot with admirable management the whole stake to one hand and total discomfiture to the other. In the negotiations with Spain we had a just claim to the Mississippi and its waters, and our citizens had a fair though very precarious claim to indemnities. We had a mere color of claim to the Rio del Norte, no claim to a line beyond the Rocky Mountains, and none to Florida, which we very much wanted. The treaty gives us the Mississippi and all its waters—gives us Florida—gives us an acknowledged line to the South Sea, and seventeen degrees of latitude upon its shores—gives our citizens five millions of dollars of indemnity—and barely gives up to Spain the colorable claim from the Sabine to the Rio del Norte. Now, negotiation implies some concession upon both sides. If after obtaining every object of your pursuit but one, and that one weak in principle and of no present value, what would you have offered to Spain to yield that also?

Trimble had no answer to this question. . . .

## 6. REFLECTIONS UPON THE
## TRANSCONTINENTAL TREATY

*[Memoirs of John Quincy Adams, IV, 274-276]*

February 22, 1819. . . . As I was going home from my
office I met Mr. Fromentin, a Senator from Louisiana, and
asked him if the treaty had been received by the Senate. He
said it had—was read, and, as far as he could judge, had been
received with universal satisfaction. It was near one in the
morning when I closed the day with ejaculations of fervent
gratitude to the Giver of all good. It was, perhaps, the most
important day of my life. What the consequences may be of
the compact this day signed with Spain is known only to the
all-wise and all-beneficent Disposer of events, who has
brought it about in a manner utterly unexpected and by
means the most extraordinary and unforeseen. Its prospects
are propitious and flattering in an eminent degree. May they
be realized by the same superintending bounty that produced
them! May no disappointment embitter the hope which this
event warrants us in cherishing, and may its future influence
on the destinies of my country be as extensive and as favorable
as our warmest anticipations can paint! Let no idle and un-
founded exultation take possession of my mind, as if I could
ascribe to my own foresight or exertions any portion of the
event. It is the work of an intelligent and all-embracing Cause.
May it speed as it has begun! for, without a continuation of
the blessings already showered down upon it, all that has been
done will be worse than useless, and vain.

The acquisition of the Floridas has long been an object
of earnest desire to this country. The acknowledgement of a
definite line of boundary to the South Sea forms a great
epocha in our history. The first proposal of it in this negotiation was my own, and I trust it is now secured beyond the

reach of revocation. It was not even among our claims by the Treaty of Independence with Great Britain. It was not among our pretensions under the purchase of Louisiana—for that gave us only the range of the Mississippi and its waters. I first introduced it in the written proposal of 31st October last, after having discussed it verbally both with Onís and De Neuville. It is the only peculiar and appropriate right acquired by this treaty in the event of its ratification. I record the first assertion of this claim for the United States as my own, because it is known to be mine perhaps only to the members of the present Administration, and may perhaps never be known to the public—and, if ever known, will be soon and easily forgotten. The provision, by the acquisition of the Floridas, of a fund for the satisfaction of claims held by citizens of the United States upon the Spanish Government, has been steadily pursued through a negotiation now of fifteen years' standing. It is of the whole treaty that which, in the case of the ratification, will have the most immediate and sensible effects. The change in the relations with Spain, from the highest mutual exasperation and imminent war to a fair prospect of tranquillity and of secure peace, completes the auspicious characters of this transaction in its present aspect, which fills my heart with gratitude unutterable to the First Cause of all. Yet let me not forget that in the midst of this hope there are seeds of fear. The ratification of Spain is yet uncertain, and may, by many possible events, be defeated. . . . A watchful eye, a resolute purpose, a calm and patient temper, and a favoring Providence, will all be as indispensable for the future as they have been for the past in the management of this negotiation. May they not be found wanting!

## 7. OREGON AND THE BRITISH CLAIMS
[*American State Papers, Class I, Foreign Relations,* V, 446-448]

[The Secretary of State to Mr. Rush]
Washington, July 22, 1823.

Sir: Among the subjects of negotiation with Great Britain which are pressing upon the attention of this Government is the present condition of the Northwest Coast of this Continent. This interest is connected, in a manner becoming from day to day more important, with our territorial rights; with the whole system of our intercourse with the Indian tribes; with the boundary relations between us and the British North American dominions; with the fur trade; the fisheries in the Pacific Ocean; the commerce with the Sandwich Islands and China; with our boundary upon Mexico; and, lastly, with our political standing and intercourse with the Russian empire. . . .

[Adams then reviews the "free and open" provision in the third article of the Anglo-American Convention of 1818 and next rejects the various Russian claims set forth in the ukase of Emperor Alexander in 1821.]

Until the Nootka Sound contest Great Britain had never advanced any claim to territory upon the Northwest Coast of America by right of occupation. Under the treaty of 1763 her territorial rights were bounded by the Mississippi. . . .

It is stated in the 52d number of the Quarterly Review, in the article upon Kotzebue's voyage, "that the whole country, from the latitude 56° 30' to the boundary of the United States, in latitude 48°, or thereabouts, is now and has long been in the actual possession of the British Northwest Company." . . .

It is not imaginable that, in the present condition of the world, *any* European nation should entertain the project of settling a *colony* on the Northwest Coast of America. That the United States should form establishments there, with views of absolute territorial right and inland communication, is not only to be expected, but is pointed out by the finger of nature, and has been for many years a subject of serious deliberation in Congress. A plan has, for several sessions, been before them for establishing a Territorial Government on the borders of the Columbia river. It will undoubtedly be resumed at their next session, and even if then again postponed there cannot be a doubt that, in the course of a very few years, it must be carried into effect. . . .

The exclusive rights of Spain to any part of the American continents have ceased. . . . Those independent nations will possess the rights incident to that condition, and their territories, will, of course, be subject to no *exclusive* right of navigation in their vicinity, or of access to them by any foreign nation.

A necessary consequence of this state of things will be, that the American continents, henceforth, will no longer be subjects of colonization. Occupied by civilized independent nations, they will be accessible to Europeans and to each other on that footing alone, and the Pacific Ocean in every part of it will remain open to the navigation of all nations, in like manner with the Atlantic.

Incidental to the condition of national independence and sovereignty, the rights of anterior navigation of their rivers will belong to each of the American nations within its own territories.

The application of colonial principles of exclusion, therefore, cannot be admitted by the United States as lawful upon any part of the Northwest Coast of America, or as belonging to any European nation. Their own settlements there, when organized as Territorial Governments, will be adapted to the freedom of their own institutions, and, as constituent parts of the Union, be subject to the principles and provisions of their constitution. . . .

If the British Northwest and Hudson's Bay Companies have any posts on the coast, as suggested in the article of the Quarterly Review above cited, the third article of the convention of October 20, 1818, is applicable to them. Mr. Middleton is authorized by his instructions to propose an article of similar import, to be inserted in a joint convention between the United States, Great Britain, and Russia, for a term of ten years from its signature. You are authorized to make the same proposal to the British Government, and, with a view to draw a definite line of demarkation for the future, to stipulate that no settlement shall hereafter be made on the Northwest Coast or on any of the islands thereto adjoining by Russian subjects south of latitude 55°, by citizens of the United States north of latitude 51°, or by British subjects either south of 51° or north of 55°. I mention the latitude of 51°, as the bound within which we are willing to limit the future settlement of the United States, because it is not to be doubted that the Columbia river branches as far north as 51°, although it is most probably not the Taconesche Tesse of Mackenzie. As, however, the line already runs in latitude 49°, to the Stony mountains, should it be earnestly insisted upon by Great Britain, we will consent to carry it in continuance on the same parallel to the sea. . . .

## 8. OREGON AND THE RUSSIAN CLAIMS

[*American State Papers, Class I, Foreign Relations,* V, 436-437]

[The Secretary of State to Mr. Middleton]
Washington, July 22, 1823.

Sir: I have the honor of inclosing, herewith, copies of a note from Baron de Tuyll, the Russian minister, recently arrived, proposing, on the part of his Majesty the Emperor of Russia, that a power should be transmitted to you to enter upon a negotiation with the ministers of his Government concerning the differences which have arisen from the imperial ukase of 4th [16th] September, 1821, relative to the Northwest Coast of America, and of the answer from this Department acceding to this proposal. A full power is accordingly inclosed, and you will consider this letter as communicating to you the President's instructions for the conduct of the negotiation.

From the tenor of the ukase, the pretensions of the Imperial Government extend to an exclusive territorial jurisdiction from the forty-fifth degree of north latitude, on the Asiatic coast, to the latitude of fifty-one north on the western coast of the American continent; and they assume the right of interdicting the *navigation* and the fishery of all other nations to the extent of one hundred miles from the whole of that coast.

The United States can admit no part of these claims. . . .

By the treaty of the 22d of February, 1819, with Spain, the United States acquired all the rights of Spain north of latitude 42°; and by the third article of the convention between the United States and Great Britain, of the 20th of October, 1818, it was agreed that any country that might be claimed by either party on the Northwest Coast of America, westward of the Stony mountains, should, together with its harbors, bays, and creeks, and the navigation of all rivers within the same, be free and open, for the term of ten years from that date, to the vessels, citizens, and subjects of the two powers, without prejudice to the claims of either party or of any other State.

You are authorized to propose an article of the same import for a term of ten years from the signature of a joint convention between the United States, Great Britain, and Russia.

The right of the United States from the forty-second to the forty-ninth parallel of latitude on the Pacific Ocean we consider as unquestionable, being founded, first, on the acquisition by the treaty of February 22, 1819, of all the rights of Spain; second, by the discovery of the Columbia river, first from sea, at its mouth, and then by land by Lewis and Clarke; and third, by the settlement at its mouth in 1811. This territory is to the United States of an importance which no possession in North America can be of to any European nation, not only as it is but the continuity of their possessions from the Atlantic to the Pacific Ocean, but as it offers their inhabitants the means of establishing hereafter water communications from the one to the other.

It is not conceivable that any possession upon the continent of North America should be of use or importance to Russia for any other purpose than that of traffic with the natives. This was, in fact, the inducement to the formation of the Russian American Company and to the charter granted them by the Emperor Paul. It was the inducement to the ukase of the Emperor Alexander. By offering free and equal access for a term of years to navigation and intercourse with the natives to Russia, within the limits to which our claims are indisputable, we concede much more than we obtain. It is not to be doubted that, long before the expiration of that time, our settlement at the mouth of the Columbia river will become so considerable as to offer means of useful commercial intercourse with the Russian settlements on the islands of the Northwest Coast.

With regard to the territorial claim, separate from the right of traffic with the natives and from any system of colonial exclusions, we are willing to agree to the boundary line within which the Emperor Paul had granted exclusive privileges to the Russian American Company, that is to say, latitude 55°.

If the Russian Government apprehend serious inconvenience from the illicit traffic of foreigners with their settlements on the Northwest Coast, it may be effectually guarded against by stipulations similar to those, a draft of which is herewith subjoined, and to which you are authorized, on the part of the United States, to agree. . . .

# CHAPTER VI

# THE MONROE DOCTRINE

The Monroe Doctrine is a statement of the tactics which Monroe and Adams deemed best suited to win a North American empire for the United States. They placed heavy emphasis on the principle that new European colonies could no longer be permitted on the continent. American officials had previously asserted this tenet; Adams notably did so during his conversation with Canning in January, 1821, and again in his notes to Great Britain and Russia in the summer of 1823. The first selection describes Adams' personal announcement of this principle to the Russian Minister in June, 1823.

With Russia checked in the Northwest, British intentions regarding the new Latin American governments became the Secretary's primary concern. The Monroe Cabinet split on the question of proper policy, but by the last days of November, 1823, Adams had won most of his points in the intra-administration debate. His realistic assessment of British and American ambitions was partly responsible for this victory and almost wholly responsible for the ultimate success of the doctrine. This assessment is outlined in the second selection. He also argued successfully for a course in dealing with the Greek Revolution which would be compatible with these policies and finally overcame Monroe's inclination to meddle in that dispute. Out of these debates emerged the second and third principles: the United States would demand that Europe refrain from interfering in the New World, and Americans would reciprocate by pledging that they would not become involved in European struggles.

On December 2 the President publicly proclaimed these principles. He also made two other important observations. First, in announcing the division of the hemispheres, Monroe did not preclude all American interference in European affairs. In the final selection in the chapter Adams outlines the circumstances which could involve the United States in conflicts outside the New World. The Monroe Doctrine was by no means an "isolationist" document.

Second, Monroe concluded his message with a *Gloria* in which he acclaimed the thesis that continued expansion infused strength and cohesiveness into the American Union. This idea had been analyzed most extensively in *Federalist* #10 thirty-five years before by James Madison, a close friend of Monroe and Adams. Monroe's stirring conclusion provided a fitting climax to this historic announcement of American imperial ambitions.

## 1. RUSSIA AND THE NON-COLONIZATION PRINCIPLE

[*Memoirs of John Quincy Adams,* VI, 157-163]

June 28, 1823. At one o'clock there was a meeting at the President's concerning the instructions to be given to Mr. Middleton [Henry Middleton, United States Minister to Russia] for the negotiation relating to the Northwest coast of America. The question was, what he should be authorized to propose or to agree to. The Emperor's Ukase asserts a right of territory to the fifty-first degree of north latitude, and interdicts the approach of foreign vessels within one hundred Italian miles of the coast. I thought no territorial right could be admitted on this continent, as the Russians appear to have no settlement upon it, except that in California. . . .

After some discussion, it was concluded that I should draft an instruction to Mr. Middleton authorizing him first to propose an article similar to that in our Convention with Great Britain of October, 1818, agreeing that the whole coast should be open for the navigation of all the parties for a definite term of years; and as there would probably be no inducement for Russia to agree to this, he should then offer to agree to a boundary line for Russia at 55°, on condition that the coast might be frequented for trade with the natives, as it has been heretofore. . . .

July 17, 1823. At the office, Baron Tuyl [Russian Minister to the United States] came, and enquired if he might inform his Government that instructions would be forwarded by Mr. Hughes [Christopher Hughes, Adams' old friend who was carrying the instructions to Middleton] to Mr. Middleton for negotiating on the Northwest Coast question. I said he might. He then manifested a desire to know as much as I was disposed to tell him as to the purport of those instructions. I told him as much as I thought prudent, as he observed that it was personally somewhat important to him to be so far confided in here as to know the general purport of what we intended to propose. I told him specially that we should contest the right of Russia to *any* territorial establishment on this continent, and that we should assume distinctly the principle that the American continents are no longer subjects for *any* new European colonial establishments. We had a conversation of an hour or more, at the close of which he said that although there would be difficulties in the negotiation, he did not foresee that they would be insurmountable.

## 2. ADAMS EVALUATES THE POSITION OF GREAT BRITAIN
[*Memoirs of John Quincy Adams,* VI, 199-204]

November 25, 1823. I made a draft of observations upon the communications recently received from the Baron de Tuyl, the Russian Minister. Took the paper, together with the statement I had prepared of what has passed between him and me, and all the papers received from him, to the President. . . . Mr. Southard just then came in, and the President sent for the other members of the Administration, Mr. Calhoun and Mr. Wirt. Mr. Crawford continues convalescent, but was not well enough to attend. . . .

The President seemed to entertain some apprehension that the republicanism of my paper might indispose the British Government to a cordial concert of operations with us. He said they were in a dilemma between their anti-Jacobin policy, the dread of their internal reformers, which made them sympathize with the Holy Allies, and the necessities of their commerce and revenue, with the pressure of their debts and taxes, which compelled them to side with South American independence for the sake of South American trade. He believed they must ultimately take this side, but if we should shock and alarm them upon the political side of the question, and the Holy Allies could hold out to them anything to appease the craving of their commercial and fiscal interest, they might go back to the allies. . . .

I replied that, at all events, nothing that we should now do would commit us to absolute war; that Great Britain was already committed more than we; that the interest of no one of the allied powers would be promoted by the restoration of South America to Spain; that the interest of each one of them was against it, and that if they could possibly agree among themselves upon a partition principle, the only possible bait they could offer to Great Britain for acceding to it was Cuba, which neither they nor Spain would consent to give her; that my reliance upon the co-operation of Great Britain rested not upon her principles, but her interest—this I thought was clear; but that my paper came in conflict with no principle which she would dare to maintain. We avowed republicanism, but we disclaimed propagandism; we asserted national independence, to which she was already fully pledged. We disavowed all interference with European affairs, and my whole paper was drawn up to come in conclusion precisely to the identical declaration of Mr. Canning himself, and to express our concurrence with it.

Mr. Southard and Mr. Wirt supported me in these remarks.

## 3. THE MONROE DOCTRINE TAKES FORM
[*Memoirs of John Quincy Adams*, VI, 177-179]

November 7, 1823. Cabinet meeting at the President's from half-past one till four. Mr. Calhoun, Secretary of War, and Mr. Southard, Secretary of the Navy, present. The subject for consideration was, the confidential proposals of the British Secretary of State, George Canning, to R. Rush [United States Minister to Great Britain], and the correspondence between them relating to the projects of the Holy Alliance upon South

America. There was much conversation, without coming to any definite point. The object of Canning appears to have been to obtain some public pledge from the Government of the United States, ostensibly against the forcible interference of the Holy Alliance between Spain and South America; but really or especially against the acquisition to the United States themselves of any part of the Spanish-American possessions.

Mr. Calhoun inclined to giving a discretionary power to Mr. Rush to join in a declaration against the interference of the Holy Allies, if necessary, even if it should pledge us not to take Cuba or the province of Texas; because the power of Great Britain being greater than ours to *seize* upon them, we should get the advantage of obtaining from her the same declaration we should make ourselves.

I thought the cases not parallel. We have no intention of seizing either Texas or Cuba. But the inhabitants of either or both may exercise their primitive rights, and solicit a union with us. They will certainly do no such thing to Great Britain. By joining with her, therefore, in her proposed declaration, we give her a substantial and perhaps inconvenient pledge against ourselves, and really obtain nothing in return. Without entering now into the enquiry of the expediency of our annexing Texas or Cuba to our Union, we should at least keep ourselves free to act as emergencies may arise, and not tie ourselves down to any principle which might immediately afterwards be brought to bear against ourselves.

Mr. Southard inclined much to the same opinion.

The President was averse to any course which should have the appearance of taking a position subordinate to that of Great Britain, and suggested the idea of sending a special Minister to *protest* against the interposition of the Holy Alliance.

I observed that it was a question for separate consideration whether we ought in any event, if invited, to attend at a Congress of the allies on this subject. . . .

I remarked that the communications recently received from the Russian Minister, Baron Tuyl, afforded, as I thought, a very suitable and convenient opportunity for us to take our stand against the Holy Alliance, and at the same time to decline the overture of Great Britain. It would be more candid, as well as more dignified, to avow our principles explicitly to Russia and France, than to come in as a cock-boat in the wake of the British man-of-war.

This idea was acquiesced in on all sides, and my draft for an answer to Baron Tuyl's note announcing the Emperor's determination to refuse receiving any Minister from the South American Governments was read. . . .

I remained with the President, and observed to him that the answer to be given to Baron Tuyl, the instructions to Mr. Rush relative to the proposals of Mr. Canning, those to Mr. Middleton at St. Petersburg, and those to the Minister who must be sent to France, must all be parts of a combined system of policy and adapted to each other; in which he fully concurred. . . .

## 4. THE TWO HEMISPHERES PRINCIPLE AND THE GREEK REVOLUTION

[*Memoirs of John Quincy Adams*, VI, 193-198]

November 21, 1823. . . . I had received a note from the President requesting me to attend a meeting of the members of the Administration at one. The meeting lasted till five. I took with me the draft of my dispatch to R. Rush in answer to Canning's proposals. . . .

I mentioned also my wish to prepare a paper to be delivered

confidentially to Baron Tuyl, and the substance of which I would in the first instance express to him in a verbal conference. It would refer to the verbal communications . . . manifested in the extract of a dispatch relating to Spanish affairs which he lately put into my hands. My purpose would be in a moderate and conciliatory manner, but with a firm and determined spirit, to declare our dissent from the principles avowed in those communications; to assert those upon which our own Government is founded, and, while disclaiming all intention of attempting to propagate them by force, and all interference with the political affairs of Europe, to declare our expectation and hope that the European powers will equally abstain from the attempt to spread their principles in the American hemisphere, or to subjugate by force any part of these continents to their will.

The President approved of this idea; and then taking up the sketches that he had prepared for his message, read them to us. Its introduction was in a tone of deep solemnity and of high alarm, intimating that this country is menaced by imminent and formidable dangers, such as would probably soon call for their most vigorous energies and the closest union. It then proceeded to speak of the foreign affairs, chiefly according to the sketch I had given him some days since, but with occasional variations. It then alluded to the recent events in Spain and Portugal, speaking in terms of the most pointed reprobation of the late invasion of Spain by France, and of the principles upon which it was undertaken by the open avowal of the King of France. It also contained a broad acknowledgment of the Greeks as an independent nation, and a recommendation to Congress to make an appropriation for sending a Minister to them.

Of all this Mr. Calhoun declared his approbation. I expressed as freely my wish that the President would reconsider the whole subject before he should determine to take that course. I said the tone of the introduction I apprehended would take the nation by surprise and greatly alarm them. It would come upon them like a clap of thunder. . . . This message would be a summons to arms—to arms against all Europe, and for objects of policy exclusively European— Greece and Spain. It would be as new, too, in our policy as it would be surprising. For more than thirty years Europe had been in convulsions; every nation almost of which it is composed alternately invading and invaded. Empires, kingdoms, principalities, had been overthrown, revolutionized, and counter-revolutionized, and we had looked on safe in our distance beyond an intervening ocean, and avowing a total forbearance to interfere in any of the combinations of European politics. This message would at once buckle on the harness and throw down the gauntlet. It would have the air of open defiance to all Europe, and I should not be surprised if the first answer to it from Spain and France, and even Russia, should be to break off their diplomatic intercourse with us. I did not expect that the quiet which we had enjoyed for six or seven years would last much longer. The aspect of things was portentous; but if we must come to an issue with Europe, let us keep it off as long as possible. Let us use all possible means to carry the opinion of the nation with us, and the opinion of the world.

Calhoun said that he thought there was not the tranquillity that I spoke of; that there was great anxiety in the thinking part of the nation; that there was a general expectation that the Holy Alliance would employ force against South America, and that it would be proper that the President should sound the alarm to the nation. A time was approaching when all its energies would be needed, and the public mind ought to be prepared for it. . . .

November 22, 1823. . . . I left with the President my draft
for a second dispatch to R. Rush on South American affairs.
And I spoke to him again urging him to abstain from everything in his message which the Holy Allies could make a
pretext for construing into aggression upon them. I said
there were considerations of weight which I could not even
easily mention at a Cabinet meeting. If he had determined
to retire from the public service at the end of his present term,
it was now drawing to a close. It was to be considered now
as a whole, and a system of administration for a definite
term of years. It would hereafter, I believed, be looked back
to as the golden age of this republic, and I felt an extreme
solicitude that its end might correspond with the character
of its progress; that the Administration might be delivered
into the hands of the successor, whoever he might be, at peace
and in amity with all the world. If this could not be, if the
Holy Alliance were determined to make up an issue with us,
it was our policy to meet, and not to make it. We should retreat to the wall before taking to arms, and be sure at every
step to put them as much as possible in the wrong. . . . The
ground that I wish to take is that of earnest remonstrance
against the interference of the European powers by force
with South America, but to disclaim all interference on our
part with Europe; to make an American cause, and adhere in-
flexibly to that. . . .

He said he would fully consider what he should say, and
when prepared with his draft would call a meeting of the
members of the Administration.

## 5. THE LAST DEBATE BEFORE THE DOCTRINE IS ANNOUNCED

*[Memoirs of John Quincy Adams, VI, 204-210]*

November 26, 1823. . . . I attended the adjourned Cabinet meeting at the President's, from half-past twelve—four hours. . . . I took a review of the preceding transactions of the Cabinet meetings; remarking that the present questions had originated in a draft which he [the President] had presented merely for consideration, of an introduction to the message, of unusual solemnity, indicating extraordinary concern, and even alarm, at the existing state of things, coupled with two paragraphs, one containing strong and pointed censure upon France and the Holy Allies for the invasion of Spain, and the other recommending an appropriation for a Minister to send to the Greeks, and in substance recognizing them as independent; that the course now proposed is a substitute for that, and that it is founded upon the idea that if an issue must be made up between us and the Holy Alliance it ought to be upon grounds exclusively American; that we should separate it from all European concerns, disclaim all intention of interfering with these, and make the stand altogether for an American cause; that at the same time the answer to be given to the Russian communications should be used as the means of answering also the proposals of Mr. George Canning, and of assuming the attitude to be maintained by the United States with reference to the designs of the Holy Alliance upon South America. This being premised, I observed that the whole of the papers now drawn up were but various parts of one system under consideration, and the only really important question to be determined, as it appeared to me, was that yesterday made by Mr. Wirt, and which had been incidentally discussed before, namely, whether we ought at all to take this attitude as regards South America; whether we get any advantage by committing ourselves to a course of opposition against the Holy Alliance. My own mind, indeed, is made up that we ought thus far to take this stand; but I thought it deserved great deliberation, and ought not to be taken without a full and serious estimate of consequences.

Mr. Wirt then resumed the objection he had taken yesterday, and freely enlarged upon it. He said he did not think this country would support the Government in a war for the independence of South America. There had never been much general excitement in their favor. Some part of the people in the interior had felt warmly for them, but it never had been general, and never had there been a moment when the people thought of supporting them by war. To menace without intending to strike was neither consistent with the honor nor the dignity of the country. It was possible that the proposals of Mr. Canning themselves were traps laid to ensnare us into public declarations against the Holy Allies, without intending even to take part against them; that if we were to be so far committed, all the documents ought to be communicated to Congress, and they ought to manifest their sentiments in the form of resolutions, and that the Executive ought not to pledge the honor of the nation to war without taking the sense of the country with them.

Mr. Calhoun supported the other view of the question. He said the great object of the measure was to detach Great Britain definitively from the Holy Alliance. Great Britain would not, could not, resist them alone, we remaining neutral. She would fall eventually into their views, and the South Americans would be subdued. The next step the allies would then take would be against ourselves—to put down what had been called the first example of successful democratic rebellion. It was probable that by taking the stand now the Holy

Alliance would be deterred from any forcible interposition with South America; but if not, we ought to sustain the ground now taken, even to the extent of war. . . .

I said, with regard to the objections of Mr. Wirt, that I considered them of the deepest moment. I was glad they had been made, and trusted the President would give them full consideration before coming to his definitive decision. If they prevailed, neither the paragraph in the message nor my draft would be proper. The draft was prepared precisely to correspond with the paragraph in the message. I did believe, however, that both would be proper and necessary. Not that I supposed that the Holy Alliance had any intention of ultimately attacking us, or meant to establish monarchy among us. But if they should really invade South America, and especially Mexico, it was impossible, in the nature of things, that they should do it to restore the old exclusive dominion of Spain. Spain had not, and never could again have, the physical force to maintain that dominion; and if the countries should be kept in subjugation by the armies of the Allies, was it in human absurdity to imagine that they should waste their blood and treasure to prohibit their own subjects upon pain of death to set foot upon those territories? Surely not. If then the Holy Allies should subdue Spanish America, however they might at first set up the standard of Spain, the ultimate result of their undertaking would be to recolonize them, partitioned out among themselves. Russia might take California, Peru, Chile; France, Mexico—where we know she has been intriguing to get a monarchy under a Prince of the House of Bourbon, as well as at Buenos Ayres. And Great Britain, as her last resort, if she could not resist this course of things, would take at least the island of Cuba for her share of the scramble. Then what would be our situation—England holding Cuba, France Mexico? . . .

There was another point of view, which the President had in part suggested, and which I thought highly important. Suppose the Holy Allies should attack South America, and Great Britain should resist them alone and without our cooperation. I thought this not an improbable contingency, and I believed in such a struggle the allies would be defeated and Great Britain would be victorious, by her command of the sea. But, as the independence of the South Americans would then be only protected by the guarantee of Great Britain, it would throw them completely into her arms, and in the result make them her Colonies instead of those of Spain. My opinion was, therefore, that we must act promptly and decisively. But the act of the Executive could not, after all, commit the nation to a pledge of war. . . .

## 6. THE MONROE DOCTRINE

President James Monroe's Seventh Annual Message, December 2, 1823

[*James D. Richardson, Messages and Papers of the Presidents,* II, 209-220]

. . . At the proposal of the Russian Imperial Government, made through the minister of the Emperor residing here, a full power and instructions have been transmitted to the minister of the United States at St. Petersburg to arrange by amicable negotiation the respective rights and interests of the two nations on the northwest coast of this continent. A similar proposal had been made by His Imperial Majesty to the Government of Great Britain, which has likewise been acceded to. The Government of the United States has been desirous by this friendly proceeding of manifesting the great value which they have invariably attached to the friendship of the

Emperor and their solicitude to cultivate the best understanding with his Government. In the discussions to which this interest has given rise and in the arrangements by which they may terminate the occasion has been judged proper for asserting, as a principle in which the rights and interests of the United States are involved, that the American continents, by the free and independent condition which they have assumed and maintain, are henceforth not to be considered as subjects for future colonization by any European powers. . . .

In the West Indies and the Gulf of Mexico our naval force has been augmented by the addition of several small vessels provided for by the "act authorizing an additional naval force for the suppression of piracy," passed by Congress at their last session. That armament has been eminently successful in the accomplishment of its object. The piracies by which our commerce in the neighborhood of the Island of Cuba had been afflicted have been repressed and the confidence of our merchants in a great measure restored. . . .

It is a source of great satisfaction that we are always enabled to recur to the conduct of our Navy with pride and commendation. As a means of national defense it enjoys the public confidence, and is steadily assuming additional importance. . . .

The sum which was appropriated at the last session for the repairs of the Cumberland road has been applied with good effect to that object. . . .

Many patriotic and enlightened citizens who have made the subject an object of particular investigation have suggested an improvement of still greater importance. They are of opinion that the waters of the Chesapeake and Ohio may be connected together by one continued canal. . . . If this could be accomplished it is impossible to calculate the beneficial consequences which would result from it. A great portion of the produce of the very fertile country through which it would pass would find a market through that channel. Troops might be moved with great facility in war. . . . Connecting the Atlantic with the Western country in a line passing through the seat of the National Government, it would contribute essentially to strengthen the bond of union itself. . . . It will likewise be proper to extend their examination to the several routes through which the waters of the Ohio may be connected by canals with those of Lake Erie. . . .

A strong hope has been long entertained, founded on the heroic struggle of the Greeks, that they would succeed in their contest and resume their equal station among the nations of the earth. It is believed that the whole civilized world take a deep interest in their welfare. Although no power has declared in their favor, yet none, according to our information, has taken part against them. Their cause and their name have protected them from dangers which might ere this have overwhelmed any other people. The ordinary calculations of interest and of acquisition with a view to aggrandizement, which mingles so much in the transactions of nations, seem to have had no effect in regard to them. From the facts which have come to our knowledge there is good cause to believe that their enemy has lost forever all dominion over them; that Greece will become again an independent nation. That she may obtain that rank is the object of our most ardent wishes.

It was stated at the commencement of the last session that a great effort was then making in Spain and Portugal to improve the condition of the people of those countries, and that it appeared to be conducted with extraordinary moderation. . . . Of events in that quarter of the globe, with which we have so much intercourse and from which we derive our origin, we have always been anxious and interested spectators. The citizens of the United States cherish sentiments the most friendly in favor of the liberty and happiness of their fellow-men on that side of the Atlantic. In the wars of the European powers in matters relating to themselves we have never taken any part, nor does it comport with our policy so to do. It is only when our rights are invaded or seriously menaced that we resent injuries or make preparation for our defense. With the movements in this hemisphere we are of necessity more immediately connected, and by causes which must be obvious to all enlightened and impartial observers. The political system of the allied powers is essentially different in this respect from that of America. This difference proceeds from that which exists in their respective Governments; and to the defense of our own, which has been achieved by the loss of so much blood and treasure, and matured by the wisdom of their most enlightened citizens, and under which we have enjoyed unexampled felicity, this whole nation is devoted. We owe it, therefore, to candor and to the amicable relations existing between the United States and those powers to declare that we should consider any attempt on their part to extend their system to any portion of this hemisphere as dangerous to our peace and safety. With the existing colonies or dependencies of any European power we have not interfered and shall not interfere. But with the Governments who have declared their independence and maintained it, and whose independence we have, on great consideration and on just principles, acknowledged, we could not view any interposition for the purpose of oppressing them, or controlling in any other manner their destiny, by any European power in any other light than as the manifestation of an unfriendly disposition toward the United States. In the war between those new Governments and Spain we declared our neutrality at the time of their recognition, and to this we have adhered, and shall continue to adhere, provided no change shall occur which, in the judgment of the competent authorities of this Government, shall make a corresponding change on the part of the United States indispensable to their security.

The late events in Spain and Portugal show that Europe is still unsettled. Of this important fact no stronger proof can be adduced than that the allied powers should have thought it proper, on any principle satisfactory to themselves, to have interposed by force in the internal concerns of Spain. To what extent such interposition may be carried, on the same principle, is a question in which all independent powers whose governments differ from theirs are interested, even those most remote, and surely none more so than the United States. Our policy in regard to Europe, which was adopted at an early stage of the wars which have so long agitated that quarter of the globe, nevertheless remains the same, which is, not to interfere in the internal concerns of any of its powers; to consider the government *de facto* as the legitimate government for us; to cultivate friendly relations with it, and to preserve those relations by a frank, firm, and manly policy, meeting in all instances the just claims of every power, submitting to injuries from none. But in regard to those continents circumstances are eminently and conspicuously different. It is impossible that the allied powers should extend their political system to any portion of either continent without endangering our peace and happiness; nor can anyone believe that our southern brethren, if left to themselves, would adopt it of their own accord. It is equally impossible, therefore, that we should behold such interposition in any form with indifference. If we look to the comparative strength and resources of Spain and those new Governments, and their distance from each other, it must be obvious that she can never subdue them. It is still the true policy of the United States to leave the parties to themselves in the hope that other powers will pursue the same course.

If we compare the present condition of our Union with its actual state at the close of our Revolution, the history of the world furnishes no example of a progress in improvement in all the important circumstances which constitute the happiness of a nation which bears any resemblance to it. At the first epoch our population did not exceed 3,000,000. By the last census it amounted to about 10,000,000, and, what is more extraordinary, it is almost altogether native, for the immigration from other countries has been inconsiderable. At the first epoch half the territory within our acknowledged limits was uninhabited and a wilderness. Since then new territory has been acquired of vast extent, comprising within it many rivers, particularly the Mississippi, the navigation of which to the ocean was of the highest importance to the original States. Over this territory our population has expanded in every direction, and new States have been established almost equal in number to those which formed the first bond of our Union. This expansion of our population and accession of new States to our Union have had the happiest effect on all its highest interests. That it has eminently augmented our resources and added to our strength and respectability as a power is admitted by all. But it is not in these important circumstances only that this happy effect is felt. It is manifest that by enlarging the basis of our system and increasing the number of States the system itself has been greatly strengthened in both its branches. Consolidation and disunion have thereby been rendered equally impracticable. Each Government, confiding in its own strength, has less to apprehend from the other, and in consequence each, enjoying a greater freedom of action, is rendered more efficient for all the purposes for which it was instituted. It is unnecessary to treat here of the vast improvement made in the system itself by the adoption of this Constitution and of its happy effect in elevating the character and in protecting the rights of the nation as well as of individuals. To what, then, do we owe these blessings? It is known to all that we derive them from the excellence of our institutions. Ought we not, then, to adopt every measure which may be necessary to perpetuate them?

## 7. THE TWO HEMISPHERES POLICY MODIFIED
[To Hugh Nelson, April 28, 1823, *The Writings of John Quincy Adams,* VII, 370-371]

. . . It has been a maxim in the policy of these United States, from the time when their independence was achieved, to keep themselves aloof from the political systems and contentions of Europe. To this principle it is yet the purpose of the President to adhere: and in the war about to commence, the attitude to be assumed and maintained by the United States will be that of neutrality.

But the experience of our national history has already shown that, however sincerely this policy was adopted, and however earnestly and perseveringly it was maintained, it yielded ultimately to a course of events by which the violence and injustice of European powers involved the immediate interests and brought in conflict the essential rights of our own country.

Two of the principal causes of the wars between the nations of Europe since that of our own Revolution, have been, indeed, the same as those in which that originated—civil liberty and national independence. To these principles, and to the cause of those who contend for them, the people of the United States can never be indifferent. . . .

In the *maritime* wars of Europe, we have, indeed, a direct and important interest of our own; as they are waged upon an element which is the common property of all; and as our participation in the possession of that property is perhaps greater than that of any other nation. The existence of maritime war, itself, enlarges and deepens the importance of this interest; and it introduces a state of things in which the conflict of neutral and belligerent rights becomes itself a continual and formidable instigation to war. To all maritime wars Great Britain can scarcely fail of becoming a party; and from that moment arises a collision between her and these states, peculiar to the situation, interests and rights of the two countries, and which can scarcely form a subject of discussion between any other nation and either of them.

This cause then is peculiarly our own: and we have already been once compelled to vindicate our rights implicated in it by war. It has been too among the dispensations of Providence, that the issue of that war should have left that question unsettled for the future; and that the attempts which on the part of the United States have been repeatedly made since the peace for adjusting it by amicable negotiation, have in like manner proved ineffectual. There is therefore great reason to apprehend, that if Great Britain should engage in the war, now just kindled in Europe, the United States will again be called to support by all their energies, not excepting war, the rights of their national independence, enjoyed in the persons of their seamen.

# CHAPTER VII

# LATIN AMERICAN REVOLUTIONS AND THE CUBAN DILEMMA

Three years after Monroe's famous message, Adams explicitly interpreted the doctrine as a device to protect and expand United States commercial interests to the south. This paper, given as the seventh selection in this chapter, climaxed a five-year change in Adams' attitude toward these new nations and displayed marked differences from the policies he had expounded in his earlier conversations with Henry Clay and in the comprehensive instructions written to the new American Minister to Colombia in 1823.

Cuba required special attention, particularly in the context of the revived slavery issue. In instructions to the United States Minister to Spain, Adams outlined his general views of both Cuba's destiny and how Americans could outmaneuver British ambitions in the Caribbean.

## 1. LATIN AMERICAN REVOLUTIONS AND HENRY CLAY

*[Memoirs of John Quincy Adams, V, 323-326]*

March 9, 1821. Mr. Clay called at the office. . . .

He said he regretted that his views had differed from those of the Administration in relation to South American affairs. He hoped, however, that this difference would now be shortly over. But he was concerned to see indications of unfriendly dispositions towards the South Americans in our naval officers who were sent to the Pacific, and he was apprehensive they would get into some quarrel there, which might alienate the minds of the people in the two countries from each other.

I said the instructions to the naval officers were as positive and pointed as words could make them to avoid everything of that kind. I hoped no such event would occur, as we could have no possible motive for quarrelling with the South Americans. I also regretted the difference between his views and those of the Administration upon South American affairs. That the final issue of their present struggle would be their entire independence of Spain I had never doubted. That it was our true policy and duty to take no part in the contest I was equally clear. The principle of neutrality to *all* foreign wars was, in my opinion, fundamental to the continuance of our liberties and of our Union. So far as they were contending for independence, I wished well to their cause; but I had seen and yet see no prospect that they would establish free or liberal institutions of government. They are not likely to promote the spirit either of freedom or order by their example. They have not the first elements of good or free government. Arbitrary power, military and ecclesiastical, was stamped upon their education, upon their habits, and upon all their institutions. Civil dissension was infused into all their seminal principles. War and mutual destruction was in every member of their organization, moral, political, and physical. I had little expectation of any beneficial result to this country from any future connection with them, political or commercial. We should derive no improvement to our own institutions by any communion with theirs. Nor was there any appearance of a disposition in them to take any political lesson from us. As to the commercial connection, I agreed with him that little weight should be allowed to arguments of mere pecuniary interest; but there was no basis for much traffic between us. They want none of our productions, and we could afford to purchase very few of theirs. Of these opinions, both his and mine, *time* must be the test; but, I would candidly acknowledge, nothing had hitherto occurred to weaken in my mind the view which I had taken of this subject from the first.

He did not pursue the discussion. . . .

## 2. ADAMS EXPLAINS AMERICAN RECOGNITION POLICY TO SPAIN, 1822

[*American State Papers, Class I, Foreign Relations,* IV, 846]

[The Secretary of State to the Minister from Spain] Washington, April 6, 1822.

Sir: Your letter of the 9th of March [protesting American recognition of several independent Latin American nations] was, immediately after I had the honor of receiving it, laid before the President of the United States, by whom it has been deliberately considered, and by whose direction I am, in replying to it, to assure you of the earnestness and sincerity with which this Government desires to entertain and to cultivate the most friendly relations with that of Spain.

This disposition has been manifested not only by the uniform course of the United States in their direct political and commercial intercourse with Spain, but by the friendly interest which they have felt in the welfare of the Spanish nation, and by the cordial sympathy with which they have witnessed their spirit and energy exerted in maintaining their independence of all foreign control and their right of self-government.

In every question relating to the independence of a nation, two principles are involved: one of *right,* and the other of *fact;* the former exclusively depending upon the determination of the nation itself, and the latter resulting from the successful execution of that determination. This right has been recently exercised, as well by the Spanish nation in Europe, as by several of those countries in the American hemisphere which had for two or three centuries been connected as colonies with Spain. In the conflicts which have attended these revolutions, the United States have carefully abstained from taking any part respecting the right of the nations concerned in them to maintain or newly organize their own political constitutions, and observing, wherever it was a contest by arms, the most impartial neutrality. But the civil war in which Spain was for some years involved with the inhabitants of her colonies in America has, in substance, ceased to exist. Treaties equivalent to an acknowledgment of independence have been concluded by the commanders and viceroys of Spain herself with the republic of Colombia, with Mexico, and with Peru; while, in the provinces of La Plata and in Chile, no Spanish force has for several years existed to dispute the independence which the inhabitants of those countries had declared.

Under these circumstances, the Government of the United States, far from consulting the dictates of a policy questionable in its morality, has yielded to an obligation of duty of the highest order, by recognizing as independent states nations which, after deliberately asserting their right to that character, had maintained and established it against all the resistance which had been or could be brought to oppose it. This recognition is neither intended to invalidate any right of Spain, nor to affect the employment of any means which she may yet be disposed or enabled to use, with the view of reuniting those provinces to the rest of her dominions. It is the mere acknowledgment of existing facts, with the view to the regular establishment with the nations newly formed of those relations, political and commercial, which it is the moral obligation of civilized and Christian nations to entertain reciprocally with one another.

It will not be necessary to discuss with you a detail of facts upon which your information appears to be materially different from that which has been communicated to this Government, and is of public notoriety. . . . The effect of the example of one independent nation upon the councils and measures of another can be just only so far as it is voluntary; and as the United States desire that their example should be followed, so it is their intention to follow that of others upon no other principle. They confidently rely that the time is at hand when all the Governments of Europe friendly to Spain, and Spain herself, will not only concur in the acknowledgment of the independence of the American nations, but in the sentiment that nothing will tend more effectually to the welfare and happiness of Spain than the universal concurrence in that recognition.

## 3. RELATIONS WITH THE NEW LATIN AMERICAN NATIONS

[*American State Papers, Class I, Foreign Relations,* V, 888-897]

[The Secretary of State to Richard C. Anderson]
Washington, May 27, 1823.

The revolution which has severed the colonies of Spanish America from European thraldom, and left them to form self-dependent Governments as members of the society of civilized nations, is among the most important events in modern history. As a general movement in human affairs it is perhaps no more than a development of principles first brought into action by the separation of these states from Great Britain, and by the practical illustration, given in the formation and establishment of our Union, to the doctrine that voluntary agreement is the only legitimate source of authority among men, and that all just Government is a compact. It was impossible that such a system as Spain had established over her colonies should stand before the progressive improvement of the understanding in this age, or that the light shed upon the whole earth by the results of our Revolution should leave in utter darkness the regions immediately adjoining upon ourselves. . . .

The European alliance of Emperors and Kings have assumed, as the foundation of human society, the doctrine of unalienable *allegiance.* Our doctrine is founded upon the principle of unalienable *right.* The European allies, therefore, have viewed the *cause* of the South Americans as rebellion against their lawful sovereign. We have considered it as the assertion of natural right. They have invariably shown their disapprobation of the revolution, and their wishes for the restoration of the Spanish power. We have as constantly favored the standard of independence and of America. In contrasting the principles and the motives of the European powers, as manifested in their policy towards South America, with those of the United States, it has not been my intention to boast of our superior purity, or to lay a claim of merit to any extraordinary favor from South America in return. Disinterestedness must be its own reward; but in the establishment of our future political and commercial intercourse with the new Republics it will be necessary to recur often to the principles in which it originated; they will serve to mark the boundaries of the rights which we may justly claim in our future relations with them, and to counteract the efforts which it cannot be doubted European negotiators will continue to make in the furtherance of their monarchical and monopolizing contemplations. . . .

The only object which we shall have much at heart in the negotiation [on commercial relations] will be the sanction by solemn compact of the broad and liberal principles of *independence, equal favors,* and *reciprocity.* . . .

There is indeed a principle of still more expansive liberality, which may be assumed as the basis of commercial intercourse between nation and nation. It is that of placing the *foreigner,* in regard to all objects of navigation and commerce, upon a footing of equal favor with the *native* citizen, and to that end, of abolishing all discriminating duties and charges whatsoever. This principle is altogether congenial to the spirit of our institutions, and the main obstacle to its adoption consists in this: that the fairness of its operation depends upon its being admitted *universally.* For while two maritime and commercial nations should bind themselves to it as a compact operative only between *them,* a third power might avail itself of its own restrictive and discriminating regulations to secure advantages to its own people, at the expense of both the parties to the treaty. The United States have, nevertheless, made considerable advances in their proposals to other nations towards the general establishment of this most liberal of all principles of commercial intercourse. . . .

Among the usual objects of negotiation in treaties of commerce and navigation are the liberty of conscience and of religious worship. Articles to this effect have been seldom admitted in Roman Catholic countries, and are even interdicted by the present constitution of Spain. The South American Republics have been too much under the influence of the same intolerant spirit; but the Colombian constitution is honorably distinguished by exemption from it. . . . Colombia will deserve new honors in the veneration of present and future ages by giving her *positive* sanction to the freedom of conscience, and by stipulating it in her first treaty with these United States. It is, in truth, an essential part of the system of American independence. Civil, political, commercial, and religious liberty, are but various modifications of one great principle, founded in the unalienable rights of human nature, and before the universal application of which the colonial domination of Europe over the American hemisphere has fallen, and is crumbling into dust. . . .

The materials of commercial intercourse between the United States and the Colombian Republic are at present not many. Our exports to it hitherto have been confined to flour, rice, salted provisions, lumber, a few manufactured articles, warlike stores, and arms, and some East India productions, for which we have received cocoa, coffee, indigo, hides, copper, and specie. Much of this trade has originated and has continued only by the war in which that country has been engaged, and will cease with it. As producing and navigating nations, the United States and Colombia will be rather competitors and rivals than customers to each other. But as navigators and manufacturers, *we* are already so far advanced in a career upon which *they* are yet to enter, that we may, for many years after the conclusion of the war, maintain with them a commercial intercourse, highly beneficial to both parties, as *carriers* to and for them of numerous articles of manufacture and of foreign produce. It is the nature of commerce, when unobstructed by interference of authority, to find its own channels and to make its own way. Let us only not undertake to regulate that which will best regulate itself. . . .

By the general *usage* of nations, independent of treaty stipulation, the property of an enemy is liable to capture in the vessel of a friend. It is not possible to justify this rule upon any sound principle of the law of nature; for by that law the belligerent party has no right to pursue or attack his enemy without the jurisdiction of either of them. The high seas are a general jurisdiction common to all, qualified by a special jurisdiction of each nation over its own vessels. As the theatre of general and common jurisdiction, the vessels of one nation and their commanders have no right to exercise over those of another any act of authority whatsoever. This is universally admitted in time of peace. War gives the belligerent a right to pursue his enemy within the jurisdiction common to both, but not into the special jurisdiction of the neutral party. If the belligerent has a right to take the property of his enemy on the seas, the neutral has a right to carry *and protect* the property of his friend on the same element. War gives the belligerent no natural right to take the property of his enemy from the vessel of his friend. But as the belligerent is armed, and the neutral, as such, is defenceless, it has grown into *usage* that the belligerent should take the property of his enemy. . . . It is evident, however, that this *usage* has no foundation in natural right, but has arisen merely from *force* used by the belligerent, and which the neutral in the origin did not resist because he had not the power. But it is a usage harsh and cruel in its operation and unjust in its nature; and it never fails in time of maritime war to produce irritation and animosity between the belligerent and the neutral. . . .

That the fabric of our social connexions with our southern neighbors may rise, in the lapse of years, with a grandeur and harmony of proportion corresponding with the magnificence of the means placed by Providence in our power, and in that of our descendants, its foundations must be laid in principles of politics and of morals new and distasteful to the thrones and dominations of the elder world, but co-extensive with the surface of the globe, and lasting as the changes of time.

## 4. THE DANGER POSED BY CUBA
*[Memoirs of John Quincy Adams, VI, 70-72]*

September 27, 1822. . . . Attended at the President's at one o'clock. Mr. Calhoun was there, Mr. Wirt being unwell and not able to attend. The proposition of Mr. Sanchez . . . was discussed. [Adams summarizes this "proposition" elsewhere in his *Memoirs:* "that the people of Cuba should immediately declare themselves independent of Spain without any co-operation of the United States, and then ask admission to the Confederation as one of the States of the Union."] There was also a second letter, explanatory of the first, and more strictly confidential. The question was discussed what was to be done. Mr. Calhoun has a most ardent desire that the island of Cuba should become a part of the United States, and says that Mr. Jefferson has the same. There are two dangers to be averted by that event: one, that the island should fall into the hands of Great Britain; the other, that it should be revolutionized by the negroes. Calhoun says Mr. Jefferson told him two years ago that we ought, at the first possible opportunity, to take Cuba, though at the cost of a war with England; but as we are not now prepared for this, and as our great object must be to gain time, he thought we should answer this overture by dissuading them from their present purpose, and urging them to adhere at present to their connection with Spain.

I thought it advisable to take a different course; to give them no advice whatever; to say that the Executive of the United States is not competent to promise them admission as a State into the Union; and that if it were, the proposal is of a nature which our relations of amity with Spain would not permit us to countenance.

Mr. Calhoun suggested that it would be proper for the President to make it a subject of a confidential communication to Congress at their next session, and he objected that if much stress should be laid upon our relations with Spain, as forbidding our acceptance of the proposal, it might be considered as indirect instigation to the declaration of independence, inasmuch as that would release us from the obligation of considering it as involving any of the rights of Spain. I replied that there would be no possibility of proceeding in the business by confidential communication to Congress: first, because there has not been one message with closed doors during the present Administration, nor, I believe, since the peace—the very notice of a secret session would raise an insatiate curiosity throughout the nation to know what could be its object; and, secondly, the proposal was of a nature which would not admit of secrecy. . . . The whole affair would be divulged in a week—perhaps in a day. . . . As to taking Cuba at the cost of a war with Great Britain, it would be well to enquire, before undertaking such a war, how it would be likely to terminate; and for the present, and for a long time to come, I held it for certain that a war with Great Britain for Cuba would result in her possession of that island, and not ours. In the present relative situation of our maritime forces, we could not maintain a war against Great Britain for Cuba. Nor did I think that a plain, distinct answer, that our relations with Spain forbid our encouragement of a proposal to annex one of her Colonies to our own Union, could be construed into an instigation to revolt. . . .

September 30, 1822. . . . [The Cubans who sponsored the Sanchez letter] ask admission at once; as one State, with full interior sovereignty of its own. I doubted the authority not only of the Executive, but of Congress, to perform this. Mr. Calhoun thought the case of Louisiana had settled the Constitutional question. But a transaction which should make an island separated from this continent by the ocean at once a member of the Union, with a representation in both Houses of Congress, would certainly be an act of more transcendent power than a mere purchase of territory contiguous to our own. . . .


## 5. CUBA AND THE LAW OF GRAVITY

[To Hugh Nelson, April 28, 1823, *The Writings of John Quincy Adams*, VII, 371-381]

. . . But in the war between France and Spain now commencing, other interests, peculiarly ours, will in all probability be deeply involved. Whatever may be the issue of this war, as between those two European powers, it may be taken for granted that the dominion of Spain upon the American continents, North and South, is irrecoverably gone. But the islands of Cuba and of Porto Rico still remain nominally and so far really dependent upon her, that she yet possesses the power of transferring her own dominion over them, together with the possession of them, to others. These islands, from their local position, are natural appendages to the North American continent; and one of them, Cuba, almost in sight of our shores, from a multitude of considerations has become an object of transcendent importance to the political and commercial interests of our Union. Its commanding position with reference to the Gulf of Mexico and the West India seas; the character of its population; its situation midway between our southern coast and the island of San Domingo; its safe and capacious harbor of the Havana, fronting a long line of our shores destitute of the same advantage; the nature of its productions and of its wants, furnishing the supplies and needing the returns of a commerce immensely profitable and mutually beneficial; give it an importance in the sum of our national interests, with which that of no other foreign territory can be compared, and little inferior to that which binds the different members of this Union together.

Such indeed are, between the interests of that island and of this country, the geographical, commercial, moral, and political relations, formed by nature, gathering in the process of time, and even now verging to maturity, that in looking forward to the probable course of events for the short period of half a century, it is scarcely possible to resist the conviction that the annexation of Cuba to our federal republic will be indispensable to the continuance and integrity of the Union itself. It is obvious however that for this event we are not yet prepared. Numerous and formidable objections to the extension of our territorial dominions beyond the sea present themselves to the first contemplation of the subject. Obstacles to the system of policy by which it alone can be compassed and maintained are to be foreseen and surmounted, both from at home and abroad. But there are laws of political as well as of physical gravitation; and if an apple severed by the tempest from its native tree cannot choose but fall to the ground, Cuba, forcibly disjoined from its own unnatural connection with Spain, and incapable of self-support, can gravitate only towards the North American Union, which by the same law of nature cannot cast her off from its bosom. . . .

An alliance between Great Britain and Spain may be one of the first fruits of this war [between Spain and France]. A guarantee of the island to Spain may be among the stipulations of that alliance; and in the event either of a threatened attack upon the island by France, or of attempts on the part of the islanders to assume their independence, a resort to the temporary occupation of the Havana by British forces may be among the probable expedients, through which it may be obtained, by concert between Britain and Spain herself. . . .

The transfer of Cuba to Great Britain would be an event unpropitious to the interests of this Union. This opinion is so generally entertained, that even the groundless rumors that it was about to be accomplished, which have spread abroad and are still teeming, may be traced to the deep and almost universal feeling of aversion to it, and to the alarm which the mere probability of its occurrence has stimulated. The question both of our right and our power to prevent it, if necessary, by force, already obtrudes itself upon our councils, and the administration is called upon, in the performance of its duties to the nation, at least to use all the means within its competency to guard against and forefend it.

It will be among the primary objects requiring your most earnest and unremitting attention, to ascertain and report to us any movement of negotiation between Spain and Great Britain upon this subject. . . .

You will not conceal from the Spanish government the repugnance of the United States to the transfer of the island of Cuba to any other power. . . . Informal and verbal communications on this subject with the Spanish Minister of Foreign Affairs will be most advisable. In casual conversation, and speaking as from your own impressions, you may suggest the hope, that if any question of transferring the island to any other power is, or shall be in agitation, it will not be withheld from your knowledge, or from ours; that the condition of Cuba cannot be changed without affecting in an eminent degree the welfare of this Union, and consequently the good understanding between us and Spain; that we should consider an attempt to transfer the island, against the will of its inhabitants, as subversive of their rights, no less than of our interests; and that, as it would give them the perfect right of resisting such transfer, by declaring their own independence, so if they should, under those circumstances, resort to that measure, the United States will be fully justified in supporting them to carry it into effect.

## 6. AMERICAN OBJECTIVES IN THE PANAMA CONGRESS

President Adams' message to the Senate of the United States, December 26, 1825

[James D. Richardson, *Messages and Papers of the Presidents*, II, 318-319]

. . . A report from the Secretary of State and copies of the correspondence with the South American Governments on this subject since the invitation given by them are herewith transmitted to the Senate. . . . It will be seen that the United States neither intend nor are expected to take part in any deliberations of a belligerent character; that the motive of their attendance is neither to contract alliances nor to engage in any undertaking or project importing hostility to any other nation.

But the South American nations, in the infancy of their independence, often find themselves in positions with reference to other countries with the principles applicable to which, derivable from the state of independenec itself, they have not been familiarized by experience. The result of this has been that sometimes in their intercourse with the United States they have manifested dispositions to reserve a right of granting special favors and privileges to the Spanish nation as the price of their recognition. At others they have actually established duties and impositions operating unfavorably to the United States to the advantage of other European powers, and sometimes they have appeared to consider that they might interchange among themselves mutual concessions of exclusive favor, to which neither European powers nor the United States should be admitted. . . . But it is believed to be of infinite moment that the principles of a liberal commercial intercourse should be exhibited to them, and urged with disinterested and friendly persuasion upon them when all assembled. . . .

The consentaneous adoption of principles of maritime neutrality, and favorable to the navigation of peace, and commerce in time of war, will also form a subject of consideration to this Congress. The doctrine that free ships make free goods and the restrictions of reason upon the extent of blockades may be established by general agreement with far more ease, and perhaps with less danger, by the general engagement to adhere to them concerted at such a meeting, than by partial treaties or conventions with each of the nations separately. An agreement between all the parties represented at the meeting that each will guard by its own means against the establishment of any future European colony within its borders may be found advisable. . . .

There is yet another subject upon which, without entering into any treaty, the moral influence of the United States may perhaps be exerted with beneficial consequences at such a meeting—the advancement of religious liberty. Some of the southern nations are even yet so far under the dominion of prejudice that they have incorporated with their political constitutions an exclusive church, without toleration of any other than the dominant sect. The abandonment of this last badge of religious bigotry and oppression may be pressed more effectually by the united exertions of those who concur in the principles of freedom of conscience. . . .

## 7. WHY THE UNITED STATES SHOULD PARTICIPATE IN THE PANAMA CONGRESS

**President Adams' Message to the House of Representatives of the United States, March 15, 1826**

[James D. Richardson, *Messages and Papers of the Presidents,* II, 330-338]

. . . With regard to the objects in which the agents of the United States are expected to take part in the deliberations of that congress, I deem it proper to premise that these objects did not form the only, nor even the principal, motive for my acceptance of the invitation. My first and greatest inducement was to meet in the spirit of kindness and friendship an overture made in that spirit by three sister Republics of this hemisphere. . . .

Without recurring to that total prostration of all neutral and commercial rights which marked the progress of the late European wars, and which finally involved the United States in them, and adverting only to our political relations with these American nations, it is observable that while in all other respects those relations have been uniformly and without exception of the most friendly and mutually satisfactory character, the only causes of difference and dissension between us and them which ever have arisen originated in those never-failing fountains of discord and irritation—discriminatons of commercial favor to other nations, licentious privateers, and paper blockades. . . .

The late President of the United States, in his message to Congress of the 2d December, 1823, while announcing the negotiation then pending with Russia, relating to the northwest coast of this continent, observed that the occasion of the discussions to which that incident had given rise had been taken for asserting as a principle in which the rights and interests of the United States were involved that the American continents, by the free and independent condition which they had assumed and maintained, were thenceforward not to be considered as subjects for future colonization by any European power. The principle had first been assumed in that negotiation with Russia. It rested upon a course of reasoning equally simple and conclusive. With the exception of the existing European colonies, which it was in nowise intended to disturb, the two continents consisted of several sovereign and independent nations, whose territories covered their whole surface. By this their independent condition the United States enjoyed the right of commercial intercourse with every part of their possessions. To attempt the establishment of a colony in those possessions would be to usurp to the exclusion of others a commercial intercourse which was the common possession of all. It could not be done without encroaching upon existing rights of the United States. The Government of Russia has never disputed these positions nor manifested the slightest dissatisfaction at their having been taken. Most of the new American Republics have declared their entire assent to them, and they now propose, among the subjects of consultation at Panama, to take into consideration the means of making effectual the assertion of that principle, as well as the means of resisting interference from abroad with the domestic concerns of the American Governments. . . .

Mindful of the advice given by the father of our country in his Farewell Address, that the great rule of conduct for us in regard to foreign nations is, in extending our commercial relations, to have with them as little political connection as possible, and faithfully adhering to the spirit of that admonition, I can not overlook the reflection that the counsel of Washington in that instance, like all the counsels of wisdom, was founded upon the circumstances in which our country and the world around us were situated at the time when it was given; that the reasons assigned by him for his advice were that Europe had a set of primary interests which to us had none or a very remote relation; that hence she must be engaged in frequent controversies, the causes of which were essentially foreign to our concerns; that our *detached* and *distant* situation invited and enabled us to pursue a different course; that by our union and rapid growth, with an efficient Government, the period was not far distant when we might defy material injury from external annoyance, when we might take such an attitude as would cause our neutrality to be respected, and, with reference to belligerent nations, might choose peace or war, as our interests, guided by justice, should counsel.

Compare our situation and the circumstances of that time with those of the present day, and what, from the very words of Washington then, would be his counsels to his countrymen now? Europe has still her set of primary interests, with which we have little or a remote relation. Our distant and detached situation with reference to Europe remains the same. But we were then the only independent nation of this hemisphere, and we were surrounded by European colonies, with the greater part of which we had no more intercourse than with the inhabitants of another planet. Those colonies have now been transformed into eight independent nations, extending to our very borders, seven of them Republics like ourselves, with whom we have an immensely growing commercial, and *must* have and have already important political, connections; with reference to whom our situation is neither distant nor detached; whose political principles and systems of government, congenial with our own, must and will have an action and counteraction upon us and ours to which we can not be indifferent if we would.

The rapidity of our growth, and the consequent increase of our strength, has more than realized the anticipations of this admirable political legacy. Thirty years have nearly elapsed since it was written, and in the interval our population, our wealth, our territorial extension, our power—physical and moral—have nearly trebled. Reasoning upon this state of things from the sound and judicious principles of Washington, must we not say that the period which he predicted as then not far off has arrived; that *America* has a set of primary interests which have none or a remote relation to Europe; that the interference of Europe, therefore, in those concerns should be spontaneously withheld by her upon the same principles that we have never interfered with hers, and that if she should interfere, as she may, by measures which may have a great and dangerous recoil upon ourselves, we might be called in defense of our own altars and firesides to take an attitude which would cause our neutrality to be respected, and choose peace or war, as our interest, guided by justice, should counsel.

The acceptance of this invitation, therefore, far from conflicting with the counsel or the policy of Washington, is directly deducible from and conformable to it. . . .

# CHAPTER VIII

# STATE-RIGHTS, SLAVERY, AND FAILURE

In the opening selection Adams observes that the success of a nation's foreign policy depends upon that nation's internal strength. During the last quarter-century of his life he dedicated himself to building a domestic system which would both preserve individual liberty and support a continental empire. This was a delicate and immense task, breath-taking in its concepts and for Adams heart-breaking in its results.

As the second selection indicates, the Missouri Compromise battle of 1820 forced him to undertake this mission. Five years later, with the powers of the presidency now in his hands, Adams tried to consolidate the system with a vast national system of internal improvements. His First Annual Message outlines this scheme. The Jacksonians had great fun with some sections of the message, such as the reference to "lighthouses of the skies," but they saw little humor in Adams' thrusts at their state-rights beliefs. Opponents had no difficulty in defeating the plan, and by 1837 Adams believed that his defeat on this issue had fatally weakened the Union, especially in its ability to deal with slavery.

After leaving the Executive Mansion, Adams turned his energies to fighting slavery, although he found small comfort in the abolitionist movement. In 1844-

1845, fighting one of his final battles in the realm of foreign affairs, Adams failed to stall the drive to annex Texas. His despair is expressed in the final selection. The war with Mexico followed a year later, forcing the nation to deal with issues which climaxed in the bloodshed of the Civil War.

=====

## 1. A STRONG FOREIGN POLICY NEEDS A STRONG UNION

[To John Adams, August 1, 1816, from England; *The Writings of John Quincy Adams,* VI, 60-62]

. . . The longer I live the stronger I find my national feelings grow upon me, and the less of my affections are compassed by partial localities. My system of politics more and more inclines to strengthen the union and its government. It is directly the reverse of that professed by Mr. John Randolph, of relying principally upon the state governments. The effort of every one of the state governments would be to sway the whole union for its own local advantage. The doctrine is therefore politic enough for a citizen of the most powerful state in the union, but it is good for nothing for the weaker states, and pernicious for the whole. But it is the contemplation of our external relations that makes me specially anxious to strengthen our national government. The conduct and issue of the late war has undoubtedly raised our national character in the consideration of the world; but we ought also to be aware that it has multiplied and embittered our enemies. This nation [England] is far more inveterate against us than it ever was before. All the restored governments of Europe are deeply hostile to us. The Royalists everywhere detest and despise us as Republicans. . . . How long it will be possible for us to preserve peace with all Europe it is impossible to foresee. Of this I am sure, that we cannot be too well or too quickly prepared for a new conflict to support our rights and our interests. The tranquillity of Europe is precarious, it is liable to many sudden changes and great convulsions; but there is none in probable prospect which would give us more security than we now enjoy against the bursting of another storm upon ourselves. I can never join with my voice in the toast which I see in the papers attributed to one of our gallant naval commanders. [Stephen Decatur had given the famous toast: "Our country! In her intercourse with foreign nations, may she always be in the right; but our country, right or wrong."] I cannot ask of heaven success, even for my country, in a cause where she should be in the wrong. *Fiat justitia, pareat coelum.* My toast would be, may our country be always successful, but whether successful or otherwise always right. I disclaim as unsound all patriotism incompatible with the principles of eternal justice. But the truth is that the American union, while united, *may* be certain of success in every rightful cause, and may if it pleases never have any but a rightful cause to maintain. They are at this moment the strongest nation upon the globe for every purpose of justice. May they be just to secure the favor of heaven, and wise to make a proper application of their strength. May they be armed in thunder for the defense of right, and self-shackled in eternal impotence for the support of wrong.

## 2. THE MISSOURI COMPROMISE AND THE MORAL RAMIFICATIONS OF SLAVERY

[*Memoirs of John Quincy Adams*, V, 3-12]

March 3, 1820. . . . And so it is that a law for perpetuating slavery in Missouri, and perhaps in North America, has been smuggled through both Houses of Congress. I have been convinced from the first starting of this question that it could not end otherwise. The fault is in the Constitution of the United States, which has sanctioned a dishonorable compromise with slavery. There is henceforth no remedy for it but a new organization of the Union, to effect which a concert of all the white States is indispensable. Whether that can ever be accomplished is doubtful. It is a contemplation not very creditable to human nature that the cement of common interest produced by slavery is stronger and more solid than that of unmingled freedom. In this instance the slave States have clung together in one unbroken phalanx, and have been victorious by the means of accomplices and deserters from the ranks of freedom. . . .

When I came this day to my office, I found there a note requesting me to call at one o'clock at the President's house. . . .

After this meeting, I walked home with Calhoun [John Calhoun of South Carolina, Secretary of War] who said that the principles which I had avowed [about constitutional rights] were just and noble; but that in the Southern country, whenever they were mentioned, they were always understood as applying only to white men. Domestic labor was confined to the blacks, and such was the prejudice, that if he, who was the most popular man in his district, were to keep a white servant in his house, his character and reputation would be irretrievably ruined.

I said that this confounding of the ideas of servitude and
labor was one of the bad effects of slavery; but he thought
it attended with many excellent consequences. It did not apply
to all kinds of labor—not, for example, to farming. He himself had often held the plough; so had his father. Manufacturing and mechanical labor was not degrading. It was
only manual labor—the proper work of slaves. No white
person could descend to that. And it was the best guarantee
to equality among the whites. It produced an unvarying
level among them. It not only did not excite, but did not
even admit of inequalities, by which one white man could
domineer over another.

I told Calhoun I could not see things in the same light.
It is, in truth, all perverted sentiment—mistaking labor for
slavery, and dominion for freedom. The discussion of this
Missouri question has betrayed the secret of their souls. In
the abstract they admit that slavery is an evil, they disclaim
all participation in the introduction of it, and cast it all upon
the shoulders of our old Grandam Britain. But when probed
to the quick upon it, they show at the bottom of their souls
pride and vainglory in their condition of masterdom. They
fancy themselves more generous and noble-hearted than the
plain freemen who labor for subsistence. They look down
upon the simplicity of a Yankee's manners, because he has
no habits of overbearing like theirs and cannot treat negroes
like dogs. It is among the evils of slavery that it taints the
very sources of moral principle. It establishes false estimates
of virtue and vice; for what can be more false and heartless
than this doctrine which makes the first and holiest rights
of humanity to depend upon the color of the skin? It perverts
human reason, and reduces man endowed with logical powers
to maintain that slavery is sanctioned by the Christian religion, that slaves are happy and contented in their condition,

that between master and slave there are ties of mutual attachment and affection, that the virtues of the master are refined and exalted by the degradation of the slave; while at the same time they vent execrations upon the slave-trade, curse Britain for having given them slaves, burn at the stake negroes convicted of crimes for the terror of the example, and writhe in agonies of fear at the very mention of human rights as applicable to men of color. . . . I have favored this Missouri compromise, believing it to be all that could be effected under the present Constitution, and from extreme unwillingness to put the Union at hazard. But perhaps it would have been a wiser as well as a bolder course to have persisted in the restriction upon Missouri, till it should have terminated in a convention of the States to revise and amend the Constitution. This would have produced a new Union of thirteen or fourteen States unpolluted with slavery, with a great and glorious object to effect, namely, that of rallying to their standard the other States by the universal emancipation of their slaves. If the Union must be dissolved, slavery is precisely the question upon which it ought to break. For the present, however, this contest is laid asleep.

### 3. FIRST ANNUAL MESSAGE. December 6, 1825
[James D. Richardson, *Messages and Papers of the Presidents,* II, 299-317]

. . . Upon this first occasion of addressing the Legislature of the Union, with which I have been honored, in presenting to their view the execution so far as it has been effected of the measures sanctioned by them for promoting the internal improvement of our country, I can not close the communication without recommending to their calm and persevering consideration the general principle in a more enlarged extent. The great object of the institution of civil government is the improvement of the condition of those who are parties to the social compact, and no government, in whatever form constituted, can accomplish the lawful ends of its institution but in proportion as it improves the condition of those over whom it is established. Roads and canals, by multiplying and facilitating the communications and intercourse between distant regions and multitudes of men, are among the most important means of improvement. But moral, political, intellectual improvement are duties assigned by the Author of Our Existence to social no less than to individual man. For the fulfillment of those duties governments are invested with power, and to the attainment of the end—the progressive improvement of the condition of the governed—the exercise of delegated powers is a duty as sacred and indispensable as the usurpation of powers not granted is criminal and odious. Among the first, perhaps the very first, instrument for the improvement of the condition of men is knowledge, and to the acquisition of much of the knowledge adapted to the wants, the comforts, and enjoyments of human life public institutions and seminaries of learning are essential. So convinced of this was the first of my predecessors in this office, now first in the memory, as, living, he was first in the hearts, of our countrymen, that once and again in his addresses to the Congresses with whom he cooperated in the public service he earnestly recommended the establishment of seminaries of learning, to prepare for all the emergencies of peace and war—a national university and a military academy. . . .

Looking back to the history only of the half century since the declaration of our independence, and observing the generous emulation with which the Governments of France, Great Britain, and Russia have devoted the genius, the intelligence, the treasures of their respective nations to the common improvement of the species in these branches of science, is it not incumbent upon us to inquire whether we are not bound by obligations of a high and honorable character to contribute our portion of energy and exertion to the common stock? . . . We have been partakers of that improvement and owe for it a sacred debt, not only of gratitude, but of equal or proportional exertion in the same common cause. Of the cost of these undertakings, if the mere expenditures of outfit, equipment, and completion of the expeditions were to be considered the only charges, it would be unworthy of a great and generous nation to take a second thought. . . .

In inviting the attention of Congress to the subject of internal improvements upon a view thus enlarged it is not my design to recommend the equipment of an expedition for circumnavigating the globe for purposes of scientific research and inquiry. We have objects of useful investigation nearer home, and to which our cares may be more beneficially applied. The interior of our own territories has yet been very imperfectly explored. . . . I would suggest the expediency of . . . a public ship for the exploration of the whole northwest coast of this continent. . . .

Connected with the establishment of an university, or separate from it, might be undertaken the erection of an astronomical observatory, with provision for the support of an astronomer, to be in constant attendance of observation upon the phenomena of the heavens, and for the periodical publication of his observations. It is with no feeling of pride as an American that the remark may be made that on the comparatively small territorial surface of Europe there are existing upward of 130 of these lighthouses of the skies, while throughout the whole American hemisphere there is not one. If we reflect a moment upon the discoveries which in the last four centuries have been made in the physical constitution of the universe by the means of these buildings and of observers stationed in them, shall we doubt of their usefulness to every nation? . . .

The spirit of improvement is abroad upon the earth. It stimulates the hearts and sharpens the faculties not of our fellow-citizens alone, but of the nations of Europe and of their rulers. While dwelling with pleasing satisfaction upon the superior excellence of our political institutions, let us not be unmindful that liberty is power; that the nation blessed with the largest portion of liberty must in proportion to its numbers be the most powerful nation upon earth, and that the tenure of power by man is, in the moral purposes of his Creator, upon condition that it shall be exercised to ends of beneficence, to improve the condition of himself and his fellow-men. While foreign nations less blessed with that freedom which is power than ourselves are advancing with gigantic strides in the career of public improvement, were we to slumber in indolence or fold up our arms and proclaim to the world that we are palsied by the will of our constituents, would it not be to cast away the bounties of Providence and doom ourselves to perpetual inferiority?

## 4. THE FAILURE OF THE INTERNAL IMPROVEMENTS PROGRAM AND THE TRIUMPH OF JACKSON

[To Charles W. Upham, February 2, 1837, *Huntington Library Quarterly,* IV (April, 1941), 381-384]

. . . I fear I have done and can do little good in the world —and my life will end in disappointment of the good which I would have done had I been permitted. The great effort of my administration was to mature into a permanent and regular

system the application of all the superfluous revenge of the
Union to internal improvement—improvement which at this
day would have afforded high wages and constant employment
to hundreds of thousands of labourers, and in which every
dollar expended would have repaid itself fourfold in the
enhanced value of the Public Lands—With this system, in
ten years from this day, the surface of the whole Union would
have been checkered over with Rail roads and Canals—It
may still be done, half a century later, and with the limping
gait of State Legislation and private adventure—I would
have done it in the administration of the Affairs of the Nation. . . . Mr. Monroe had yielded up the narrow jealousies
and envious cringing of Jefferson's blighting breath, and
when I came to the Presidency, the principle of internal improvement, was swelling the tide of public prosperity, till
the Sable Genius of the South, saw the signs of his own in-
evitable downfall in the unparalleled progress of the general
welfare of the North, and fell to cursing the tariff, and internal improvement, and raised the Standard of Free trade,
Nullification and State Rights—I fell, and with me fell, I fear
never to rise again, certainly never to rise again in my day,
the system of internal improvement by national means and
National energies—The great object of my life therefore as
applied to the administration of the Government of the
United States has *failed*—The American Union as a moral
Person in the family of Nations, is to live from hand to mouth,
to cast away, instead of using for the improvement of its own
condition, the bounties of Providence, and to raise to the
summit of Power a succession of Presidents the consummation
of whose glory will be to growl and snarl with impotent fury
against a money broker's shop, to rivet into perpetuity the
clanking chain of the Slave, and to waste in boundless bribery
to the west the invaluable inheritance of the Public Lands.

## 5. "I WALK ON THE EDGE OF A PRECIPICE"
[*Memoirs of John Quincy Adams,* IX, 365]

Philadelphia, September 1, 1837. . . . I then went to the Anti-Slavery office, 223 Arch Street; thence to Samuel Webb's house, and afterwards to Benjamin Lundy's office. I saw and had long conversations with them both. . . . Lundy returned with me to my lodgings. He and the abolitionists generally are constantly urging me to indiscreet movements, which would ruin me and weaken and not strengthen their cause. My own family, on the other hand—that is, my wife and son and Mary—exercise all the influence they possess to restrain and divert me from all connection with the abolitionists and with their cause. Between these adverse impulses my mind is agitated almost to distraction. The public mind in my own district and State is convulsed between the slavery and abolition questions, and I walk on the edge of a precipice in every step that I take.

## 6. THE APOPLEXY OF THE CONSTITUTION
[*Memoirs of John Quincy Adams,* XII, 173-174]

February 28, 1845. The day passes, and leaves scarcely a distinct trace upon the memory of anything, and precisely because, among numberless other objects of comparative insignificance, the heaviest calamity that ever befell myself and my country was this day consummated. Immediately after the meeting of the House, the joint resolutions of the House for the admission of Texas as a State into this Union were returned from the Senate, with an amendment consisting of two additional resolutions. . . .

I regard it as the apoplexy of the Constitution.

# A BIBLIOGRAPHY

Adams' disciplined mind and inimitable style can best be appreciated in the *Memoirs,* edited by C. F. Adams in a twelve-volume edition (Philadelphia, 1874-1877), and in the *Writings of John Quincy Adams,* edited in seven volumes by Worthington C. Ford (New York, 1913-1917). The *Writings,* unfortunately, stop at the end of 1823. Allan Nevins has edited the *Memoirs* in a good one-volume edition (New York, 1929, 1951). Most of Adams' important state papers are in *American State Papers, Class I, Foreign Relations,* particularly volumes IV and V; volume III contains some of his despatches when he was American Minister abroad during the 1809-1817 period. For the early period, his *Letter to the Hon. Harrison Gray Otis . . . On the Present State of Our National Affairs* (Boston, 1808) is Adams' defense of his course in the Senate and is available in many libraries. For the later period, *Letters From John Quincy Adams to His Constituents of the Twelfth Congressional District in Massachusetts* (Boston, 1837) includes perhaps Adams' best statement on the right of petition and the threat posed by slavery to all civil liberties.

The best biography is Samuel Flagg Bemis' masterful two-volume study, *John Quincy Adams and the Foundations of American Foreign Policy* (New York, 1949), and *John Quincy Adams and the Union* (New York, 1956). Robert A. East has revealed the conflicting drives and frustrations in the young Adams in *John Quincy Adams, The Critical Years: 1785-1794* (New York, 1962). Dexter Perkins has provided a good short sketch in "John Quincy Adams" in *American Secretaries of State and Their Diplomacy,* edited by Samuel Flagg Bemis (New York, 1928). George A. Lipsky has examined

Adams' ideas topically in *John Quincy Adams: His Theory and Ideas* (New York, 1950). A moving tribute by a famous contemporary, and a disciple of Adams, is William H. Seward's *Life and Public Services of John Quincy Adams* (Auburn, New York, 1850). Other good contemporary accounts are Thomas Hart Benton's, *Thirty Years View*, 2 vols. (New York, 1854-1856); and "Correspondence of the Russian Ministers in Washington, 1818-1825," *American Historical Review*, XVIII (January, April, 1913), 309-345, 537-562. Worthington C. Ford has provided the best account of Adams' failure in having his internal improvements scheme adopted: "A Last Opportunity: Internal Improvements," *Indiana Historical Society Publications*, VI (1919), 55-81. But Adams' grandson, Brooks Adams, has caught the drama and the tragedy of this failure in his eloquent introduction to Henry Adams, *The Degradation of the Democratic Dogma* (New York, 1920).

Several books provide the context for Adams' diplomacy: George Dangerfield's well-written *The Era of Good Feelings* (New York, 1952); Albert K. Weinberg's sweeping *Manifest Destiny* (Baltimore, 1935); William Appleman Williams' stimulating interpretative study, *The Contours of American History* (Cleveland and New York, 1961); and Richard W. Van Alstyne's excellent *The Rising American Empire* (New York, 1960). The last two are good on the background of the Monroe Doctrine and complement Dexter Perkins' *The Monroe Doctrine, 1823-1826* (Cambridge, Mass., 1927); and Arthur Preston Whitaker, *The United States and the Independence of Latin America, 1800-1830* (Baltimore, 1941), which remains the best work on United States-Latin American relations in this era. Other helpful specialized studies are Frederick Merk, *Albert Gallatin and the Oregon Problem* (Cambridge, Mass., 1950); and Vernon G. Setser, *The Commercial Reciprocity Policy of the United States, 1774-1829* (Philadelphia, 1937).

# INDEX